Ignite Your Online Coaching Business:

Proven Strategies to Boost Your Income as a Health and Fitness Coach

Joe Olive

For Bee.

You were looking for someone to inspire you, and you inspired me.
Nothing is impossible when I know you believe in me.
You're my engine for impact.

YAE. WAE. HEA.

Table of Contents

Letter from the Author: Ignition - Transforming Your Coaching Business......4
Chapter 1: The Coaching Mindset: Embracing Failure as a Tool for Growth......8
Chapter 2: Understanding Your "Why": Defining Your Coaching Purpose......13
Chapter 3: The Power of Authenticity in Coaching......21
Chapter 4: Systemizing Success: Creating Efficient Processes......30
Chapter 5: The Automation Advantage: Enhancing Client Relationships......39
Chapter 6: Mastering Content Batching for Consistent Marketing......47
Chapter 7: Leveraging Data for Strategic Decision-Making......55
Chapter 8: The Art of Virtual Group Coaching......63
Chapter 9: Customizing CRM Systems for Optimal Client Management......76
Chapter 10: Strategic Outsourcing: Focusing on Your Core Competencies......83
Chapter 11: Self-Care Practices for Coaches: Avoiding Burnout......90
Chapter 12: Continuous Learning: Staying Ahead in a Dynamic Industry......97
Chapter 13: Leadership - Building an Empire, Not a Prison......103
Chapter 14: Culture: Building a Fucking Empire, Not Just a Business......110
Chapter 15: Crush Invisible Losses and Optimize Your Empire......116
Chapter 16: The Pitfalls of Premature Scaling......122
Chapter 17: Driving Growth Through Lead Generation and Sales......129
Chapter 18: Sustainable Growth and Building a Resilient Coaching Business......138
Conclusion: Your Roadmap to Coaching Success......144
Appendix: Essential Resources for Online Health and Fitness Coaches......149

Letter from the Author: Ignition - Transforming Your Coaching Business

"The secret of change is to focus all of your energy not on fighting the old, but on building the new." — Socrates

Listen up, coach. You picked up this book because you're ready for change. You've got the basics down, but you're hungry for more. You're not just looking to survive in the online coaching world – you're here to thrive.

You became a fitness professional to change lives, right? To help people transform their bodies, boost their confidence, and become the best versions of themselves. But somewhere along the way, you realized something:

Being a great coach doesn't automatically translate to running a successful coaching business.

You're working your ass off, pouring your heart and soul into your clients, but your bank account doesn't reflect your effort. You're stuck in the hamster wheel of one-on-one sessions, drowning in admin work, and wondering if you made a mistake choosing this path.

Sound familiar?

Well, buckle up. Because in this book, we will tackle the health and fitness coach's dilemma head-on. We will transform you from a hardworking coach into a savvy business owner, from someone who trades hours for dollars into someone who builds systems that generate revenue while they sleep.

This book isn't about working harder. It's about working harder at working smarter. It's about leveraging modern tools and strategies to boost your impact and income without burning out.

I've been where you are. I've overcome a toxic lifestyle, transformed my health, and navigated the treacherous waters of building a digital business. I've made the mistakes, so you don't have to.

In the pages that follow, you'll learn:

- How to develop a mindset that turns failures into fuel for growth
- Strategies to streamline your workflow and reclaim your time
- Techniques to attract high-quality clients who are ready to invest in their transformation
- Methods to scale your business without sacrificing the quality of your coaching

But here's the kicker: This isn't just about systems and strategies. It's about authenticity. In today's world, being real is your secret weapon. We're going to harness that power to build a coaching business that stands out in a crowded market.

This book is crafted for you—the coach already making strides with your business but feeling the pinch of prolonged hours and personal sacrifice. It aims to equip you with a strategic knowledge base to evolve your processes, better manage your client load, and approach change efficiently, handle sales, and increase your earnings while preserving your well-being.

We'll also discuss the value of working with your own business coach. Expert guidance can help you avoid common mistakes and fast-track your growth. By learning from the successes and failures of others, you can accelerate your journey towards the next level.

Are you ready to stop struggling and start dominating? To build a business that matches your passion and expertise? To create sustainable growth without falling into the "sell, sell, sell" trap?

Then let's fucking go. Your empire awaits.

Chapter 1: The Coaching Mindset: Embracing Failure as a Tool for Growth

In the world of online coaching, the difference between success and stagnation often boils down to one crucial factor: mindset. As a coach, developing a growth mindset—viewing challenges and failures as opportunities for learning and improvement—can be transformative, both for your business and your client relationships.

I learned this lesson the hard way. Early in my coaching career, I approached each client interaction with the pressure of needing to have all the answers. Every question I couldn't immediately answer felt like a failure. This fixed mindset not only stressed me out but also limited my ability to truly connect with and help my clients.

The turning point came when I realized that admitting "I don't know, but I'll find out" actually strengthened my client relationships rather than weakened them. This shift in perspective opened up a whole new world of possibilities.

A growth mindset, a term popularized by psychologist Carol Dweck, is the belief that abilities and intelligence can be developed through dedication, hard work, and perseverance. This stands in stark contrast to a fixed mindset, which assumes that our abilities are static and unchangeable. The implications of these mindsets are profound, especially in the coaching industry where continuous learning and adaptation are key to success.

Imagine two coaches: Alex and Taylor. Both are equally skilled and passionate about helping their clients achieve their fitness goals. However, their mindsets set them on vastly different paths.

Coach Alex, with his fixed mindset, believes that his coaching abilities are innate and unchangeable. When faced with a difficult client or a business setback, he sees it as a personal failure, a confirmation of his limitations. Discouraged, he avoids taking on new challenges and sticks to familiar routines, missing out on opportunities for growth and improvement.

On the other hand, Coach Taylor embraces a growth mindset. She views each challenge as an opportunity to learn and grow. When a client leaves or a marketing campaign fails, she doesn't see it as a personal flaw but as a chance to gather feedback, analyze what went wrong, and improve. Over time, Taylor's approach leads her to develop innovative strategies, build stronger client relationships, and grow her business in ways Alex can only dream of.

The power of embracing failure as a tool for growth extends beyond just client interactions. It permeates every aspect of running a successful coaching business. Take my own journey, for instance. When I first attempted to scale my business by hiring a team, I made countless mistakes. I hired too quickly, delegated poorly, made rushed financial decisions, and nearly ran my business into the ground.

Instead of giving up, I chose to view this setback as a valuable learning experience. I studied successful business models, sought mentorship, and knew how to build a business with a more strategic approach. Today, I know my team is one of my greatest assets, allowing me to serve more clients and make a bigger impact than I ever could alone.

To embrace growth, start by shifting your perspective. Instead of seeing failure as a negative outcome, view it as feedback. Ask yourself: What can I learn from this experience? How can I use this information to improve? This mindset shift can help you stay motivated and resilient in facing challenges.

Adopting a growth mindset doesn't happen overnight. It requires conscious effort and consistent practice.

Here are some strategies to help you develop and maintain a growth mindset in your coaching business:

1. Set realistic and challenging goals:

Break down large goals into smaller, manageable tasks. This will make the process less overwhelming and allow you to celebrate small wins along the way.

2. Practice self-reflection and mindfulness:

Regularly reflect on your experiences and identify lessons learned. Keeping a journal can be a powerful tool for self-reflection, helping you track your growth and pinpoint areas for improvement.

3. Seek feedback and learn from others:

Actively seek feedback from clients and peers. Constructive criticism is invaluable for growth. It provides insights you might not see on your own and helps you refine your approach.

Remember, embracing failure doesn't mean seeking it out or celebrating mistakes. It means approaching setbacks with curiosity rather than fear, and using them as stepping stones to improvement rather than roadblocks to success.

As we move forward in this book, keep this growth mindset at the forefront. It will be the foundation upon which we build all other strategies and tactics. In the next chapter, we'll explore how to define your unique coaching purpose, a task that becomes much more powerful when approached with a mindset of growth and continuous improvement.

Your journey to building a thriving coaching business starts with your mindset. Are you ready to embrace the challenges, learn from the setbacks, and grow in ways you never thought possible? Let's take this first crucial step together.

Chapter 2: Understanding Your "Why": Defining Your Coaching Purpose

In the competitive world of online health and fitness, having a clear sense of purpose is crucial. It's not just about standing out in a crowded market; it's about fueling your passion, driving your business decisions, and inspiring your clients. Your "why" is the foundation of your coaching business.

I learned this lesson through my diverse professional journey, which took me from the bustling world of New York City's developer consulting to the dynamic realm of health and fitness coaching. As the VP/COO of a developer consulting firm in NYC, I had it all figured out. We were helping businesses grow and managing operations during the process of constructing their new buildings efficiently, but our purpose wasn't always clearly defined.

Then COVID hit, and our business world turned upside down. Clients were pulling back, and the future looked uncertain. During this tumultuous time, I realized we had been operating without a clear "why." Sure, we were helping businesses, but to what end? What was our true impact?

This crisis forced me to dig deep and examine our motivations. Why did we start this business in the first place? What kind of impact did we truly want to make? The answers to these questions weren't just enlightening; they were transformative.

As we navigated the challenges of the pandemic, I found myself drawn to the world of health and fitness. I had my physical transformation, and it was pulling me in beyond just that. The resilience and adaptability of this industry during such trying times fascinated me. I transitioned into a sales and marketing role for a leading team in this space, and it was here that I truly understood the power of a clear, compelling "why."

In the fitness coaching world, I saw firsthand how coaches with a strong purpose thrived, even in challenging times. They weren't just selling workouts or meal plans; they offered transformation, empowerment, and a path to better lives. This clarity of purpose resonated deeply with clients, driving engagement and results. I started as a client. My journey continued as part of the staff but mostly it felt like a family.

As I embark on my journey as a business coach in the health and fitness industry, I'm bringing together my operational expertise from my developer consulting days and the insights I've gained from the fitness world. This unique combination has shaped my understanding of what it truly means to have a powerful "why" in business.

Your "why" is more than just a catchy tagline or a mission statement. It's the core reason behind your coaching—the driving force that gets you up in the morning and keeps you going when times get tough. It defines your mission, your values, and the impact you want to make in the world.

Now, plenty of people in the fitness industry are pretenders. They talk about mantras and "doing the right thing," only to be a completely different person when no one is looking. Don't just write your mantra or mission statement because it sounds cool, and one of your mentors told you to. Do it because you believe in it. Do it because you want to live it. Do it because if you truly embody the message. You will succeed if you approach it as a way of life instead of another task on your list.

Consider the story of Alex, a fitness industry coach. He started with a generic goal of helping people get fit. But as we delved deeper into his motivations, he realized his true passion was assisting busy professionals in reclaiming their health and vitality, something he had observed was crucial in his previous corporate career.

This clarity of purpose transformed Alex's business. His marketing messages became more focused and resonant. He attracted clients who were deeply aligned with his mission, leading to better results and more satisfying coaching relationships. Alex's clear "why" became the cornerstone of his success, influencing everything from his program design to pricing strategy.

So, how do you uncover your own powerful "why"? It starts with introspection and self-reflection.

Here are some strategies to help you dig deep:

1. Examine Your Journey:

Look at your own path in business and entrepreneurship. What challenges have you overcome? What transformations have you experienced? Often, our most powerful "why" comes from our personal struggles and triumphs.

2. Identify Your Values:

What principles are non-negotiable for you? Is it integrity, innovation, efficiency, or empowerment? Those are mine. Find yours. Your core values should align closely with your coaching purpose.

3. Envision Your Ideal Impact:

What would it be if you could wave a magic wand and change one thing in the coaching world? This can give you clues about the unique contribution you want to make.

4. Ask the Tough Questions:

Why did you really become a coach? What keeps you going on tough days? What kind of legacy do you want to leave? Be brutally honest with yourself.

Once you've reflected on these points, it's time to craft your purpose statement. This isn't a marketing slogan; it's a clear, concise articulation of why you do what you do. Here's a simple formula to get you started:

"I help [specific group] to [achieve specific outcome] so that [larger impact]."

For example: "I help ambitious online health and fitness coaches streamline their operations and scale their businesses so they can make a bigger impact without burning out."

Remember, this is a process. Your "why" may evolve as you grow and gain more experience. The key is to start with something authentic and meaningful to you. If you have already done this exercise, do it again every now and then. You will be surprised by what happens as you learn some things about who you are and what your business is here for.

A well-defined "why" isn't just feel-good fluff—it has tangible benefits for your coaching business:

- It guides your business decisions, helping you focus on what truly matters.
- It attracts ideal clients who resonate with your mission.
- It differentiates you in a crowded market.
- It provides motivation during challenging times.
- It inspires trust and loyalty in your clients.

My own journey from developer consulting through the challenges of COVID to finding purpose in the world of health and fitness has taught me the invaluable importance of a clear "why." It allows you to pivot when necessary, stay resilient in the face of challenges, and continually evolve your business in alignment with your core values and goals.

As you move forward in your coaching journey, let your "why" be your north star. Use it to guide your decisions, from the clients you take on to the programs you create. Let it infuse every aspect of your business, from your marketing messages to your coaching style.

In the next chapter, we'll explore leveraging authenticity in your coaching practice—a natural extension of understanding your "why." But for now, take some time to reflect on your purpose. It's the foundation upon which you'll continue to build your coaching empire.

Remember, in a world where many coaches are just going through the motions, having a clear, compelling "why" sets you apart. Don't just do it because I told you to. Do it because you want to. If you can't see the difference, just put the book down now and continue your journey without guidance. I'm not just spinning your wheels. It's what will turn your coaching business from just another job into a true calling.

Reflection Questions:

1. What experiences in your business career have shaped your passion for coaching?

2. If you could solve one problem in the online health and fitness coaching world, what would it be?

3. How does your current approach align (or not align) with your core values?

Action Steps:

1. Write down your professional journey, noting key turning points that led you to health and fitness coaching.

2. List your top 5 non-negotiable values and how they relate to your coaching business.

3. Draft your purpose statement using the formula provided.

Download the free printable PDF workbook with ALL the Action Steps, additional guides, templates and MORE:

http://engineforimpact.com/workbook

Chapter 3: The Power of Authenticity in Coaching

Listen up, coach. Authenticity is your secret weapon in this world of Instagram filters and carefully curated online personas. It's not just about being "real" – it's about being unapologetically you in every aspect of your coaching business.

I learned that trying to be someone you're not is exhausting and ineffective. In my developer consulting days, I had to fit a certain mold to be taken seriously—suits, jargon, hide my tattoos, the whole nine yards. But you know what? It felt like wearing a mask. If I'm being honest, I chose this current path because I feel I can be myself in the health and fitness industry. I don't need to be stuffy and afraid to throw around some honesty. I can be professional and me at the same time. I needed the right industry. Hello, health and fitness industry.

It wasn't until I embraced my true self – direct, no-bullshit approach and all – that I started to see real success. And let me tell you that authenticity became even more crucial when I transitioned into the health and fitness world.

In this industry, many coaches are trying to project a perfect image. Six-pack abs, perfect diets, never a hair out of place. But here's the truth: people don't connect with perfection. They connect with humanity, with struggle, with real stories of overcoming challenges.

Remember my own fitness transformation? It wasn't a smooth journey. There were setbacks, moments of doubt, and times when I wanted to throw in the towel. But sharing those struggles authentically resonates with people, building trust and connection. It is not because I am forcing it but because that is how humans work. People want to know the real you when you're creating value they choose to invest time into. It isn't rocket science.

So, what does authenticity in coaching really mean?

1. Being Honest About Your Journey:

Don't sugarcoat your story. If you struggled with weight loss, admit it. If you're still working on certain aspects of your fitness, own it. Do not emit a story of "perfection" 24/7. Your clients will appreciate your honesty and relate to your ongoing journey. They will want to be involved with you because they will know who you are at every turn. Don't embellish. Be the *real* you.

2. Showing Your Personality:

Stop trying to fit some cookie-cutter mold of what a "professional coach" should be. If you're sarcastic, be sarcastic. If you're a bit of a nerd, let that flag fly. Your unique personality is what will attract the right clients to you. It will also set you apart from the millions of other coaches online, giving everyone the same information. Be yourself.

3. Admitting When You Don't Know:

You're not all-knowing, and pretending to be is a fast track to losing credibility. When you don't have an answer, say so. Then, commit to finding out and get back to the client promptly. Your clients will respect your honesty and your dedication to growth.

4. Being Consistent Across All Platforms:

Your Instagram persona shouldn't be different from how you are in one-on-one sessions or how you write your emails. Consistency builds trust. Period.

5. Sharing Both Victories and Failures:

Celebrate your wins, absolutely. But don't shy away from sharing your setbacks, too. Your resilience in the face of challenges will inspire your clients. Be better, do better, and they will follow you on that path. Every time.

Now, I can already hear some of you thinking, "But if I'm too real, won't I scare away potential clients?" Let me be clear: authenticity isn't about oversharing or being unprofessional. It's about being genuine and relatable while still maintaining boundaries.

Here's a personal example: When I first started in high-ticket fitness coaching sales, I was tempted to hide the fact that I came from a completely different industry. I thought it might make me seem less credible. But you know what? Embracing that part of my story – how I transitioned from the corporate world to fitness – actually became one of my strongest selling points. It helped me connect with clients looking to make big life changes.

Authenticity also plays a crucial role in your marketing. In a world of copycat content and regurgitated advice, your authentic voice will cut through the noise. Don't be afraid to have opinions, challenge the status quo, or be a bit controversial if that's true to who you are. But remember to toe the line without crossing it. Easier said than done. I saw a coach or two throw politics or religion into their message too strongly and lose more than a few clients. Be you, but remember, you can be you without forcing your beliefs on others. It's actually simple. You want people to want to be like you, but that doesn't mean they need to think like you in every single way.

But here's the kicker – and pay attention because this is important – authenticity isn't a marketing strategy. It's a way of being. You're missing the point entirely if you're only "authentic" when the camera's rolling or writing a social media post.

Real authenticity means being true to yourself and your values, even when it's hard. It means turning down a high-paying client if they're not aligned with your mission. It means admitting to a mistake, even if it might make you look bad in the short term. It means staying true to your "why" even when an easier path presents itself.

So, how do you cultivate authenticity in your coaching practice?

1. Get Clear on Your Values:

Revisit your "why" and core values regularly. Let them guide you in every business decision.

2. Practice Vulnerability:

Share your own ongoing fitness journey, including the ups and downs. Let your clients see that you're human too.

3. Develop Your Unique Voice:

Stop trying to sound like every other coach out there. Write and speak in a way that's natural to you, even if it doesn't sound "too professional" by traditional standards.

4. Be Consistent:

Ensure that how you present yourself online matches who you are in real life. No Jekyll and Hyde syndrome allowed.

5. Stand for Something:

Don't be afraid to share your opinions on industry issues. Your stance might repel some, but it will strongly attract those who align with your values.

Remember, authenticity isn't about being perfect. It's about being real, being consistent, and being true to yourself and your values. It's about showing up as your full self, flaws and all, and using your unique experiences and perspective to serve your clients better.

In an industry full of smoke and mirrors, authenticity is your superpower. Use it wisely and consistently, and watch as it transforms not just your business but also the lives of your clients.

Reflection Questions:

1. In what areas of your coaching business do you feel you're not being fully authentic? Why?

2. What parts of your story or personality have you hesitated to share? How might sharing these elements actually strengthen your coaching?

3. How can you bring more of your authentic self into your marketing and client interactions?

Action Steps:

1. Write down three unique aspects of your personality or experience that you've hesitated to share. Brainstorm ways to incorporate these into your coaching.

2. Review your marketing materials. Are they truly reflective of your voice and values? If not, rewrite one piece in a way that feels more authentically you.

3. Share a personal story of struggle or failure related to fitness with your audience this week. Notice how it impacts your engagement and connection with clients.

Download the free printable PDF workbook with ALL the Action Steps, additional guides, templates and MORE:

http://engineforimpact.com/workbook

Chapter 4: Systemizing Success: Creating Efficient Processes

Listen up, coach. You've got your mindset right, you know your "why," and you're embracing authenticity. But here's the cold, hard truth: None of that matters if you can't deliver consistently. It's time to talk about systems and processes – the unsexy but crucial backbone of any successful coaching business.

Now, I know what you're thinking. "Systems? Processes? That sounds boring as hell." And you know what? You're not entirely wrong. But let me tell you something I learned the hard way: Without solid systems, you're just spinning your wheels, flying blind, and working your ass off without seeing the results you truly deserve.

Back in my NYC consulting days, I saw firsthand how the right systems could make or break a project. We're talking multi million-dollar buildings here – you can't wing it. Every step, from initial planning to final inspection, had to be methodical and repeatable. And guess what? The same principle applies to your coaching business.

When I transitioned to the fitness world, I was shocked at how many coaches were flying by the seat of their pants. No wonder they were burning out! They were reinventing the wheel with every client, every email, every ad, every social media post. It was exhausting just watching them.

So, let's break this down. What do I mean by systems and processes? I'm talking about creating repeatable, scalable ways of doing things in your business. From onboarding new clients to delivering your coaching, from content creation to follow-ups – everything should have a system.

Here's why this matters:

1. Consistency:

Systems ensure that every client gets the same high-quality experience every single time. No more forgetting important steps or dropping balls. From onboarding to exit interviews, it all matters.

2. Efficiency:

Once you have systems in place, you'll be amazed at how much time you save. Tasks that used to take hours will be done in minutes.

3. Scalability:

Want to grow your business? Good luck doing that without systems. Proper processes allow you to handle more clients without working more hours. Time is money. Every second you save is another dollar you make and, inevitably, a higher impact on your clients.

4. Freedom:

This is the big one. With the right systems, your business can run smoothly even when you're not there. Imagine taking multiple vacations throughout the year without your business falling apart. That's the power of sound systems.

I'm not saying you must turn into some robotic, process-obsessed monster. Remember, we talked about authenticity. Your systems should enhance your ability to be you, not restrict it. Think of them as the backstage crew that allows you to shine on stage.

Let's get practical. Here are some key areas where you need to implement systems:

1. Client Onboarding:

Create a step-by-step process for welcoming new clients. From the initial welcome email to gathering all necessary information, make it smooth and professional. First impressions matter, folks.

2. Content Creation:

Don't wait for inspiration to strike. Have a system for regularly creating and scheduling content. Use tools like content calendars and batching to stay ahead of the game. We will dive further into this later in the book.

3. Coaching Delivery:

Whether it's one-on-one or group coaching, have a clear structure. What happens in each session? How do you track progress? How often do you check in? Systematize it.

4. Follow-ups:

Don't let leads or current clients fall through the cracks. Set up automated reminders and have templates ready for different scenarios.

5. Financial Management:

From invoicing to expense tracking, get this shit organized. Trust me, your future self (and accountant) will thank you. A Google Sheet that you check every few months doesn't cut it. There are better ways. Make it a point to find them, learn them, and use them.

Now, here's a personal story. When I first started in high-ticket fitness coaching sales, I was a mess. I was working around the clock, constantly stressed about forgetting something important. Then I remembered my consulting days and got my act together. I started to track and systematize my own daily work.

I created a system that tracked everything from initial contact to ongoing progress. I set up email templates for common situations. I even created a follow up task tracking system that allowed me to pump out consistent, high-quality daily sales conversations without killing myself.

The result? My close rate went up, and my stress went down. I actually had more time to connect with our clients. And you know what? That's when I started seeing real results for my well-being and my bank account.

But here's the thing – and pay attention because this is crucial – systems are not set-it-and-forget-it. They need to evolve as your business grows. Input Text: What works for you now might not work when you have 100 clients, or 1000 clients. Be prepared to review and refine your processes regularly. In today's constantly evolving digital world, you're doing it very wrong if you're not constantly seeking the next best solution.

Also, don't fall into the trap of over-systemizing. The goal is to free up your time and mental energy, not to create busy work. If a system isn't serving you or your clients after an extended amount of time, ditch it or change it.

How do you start systemizing your coaching business?

1. Audit Your Current Processes:

Look at how you're currently doing things. Where are the

bottlenecks? What tasks are eating up too much of your time?

2. Identify Repetitive Tasks:

These are prime candidates for systemization. If you're doing something more than once a day, it needs a system.

3. Create Standard Operating Procedures (SOPs):

Write down step-by-step instructions for each process. Make it so clear that anyone could follow it. Do not ask other people on your team to do this for you. You need to know how it works and why. You are the backbone. Be the backbone. Delegate things later based on this SOP. This is how you end up with a team that knows they can depend on you to understand what is happening. You literally wrote the "book" on it.

4. Leverage Technology:

Use tools like CRMs, project management software, and automation platforms. They're game-changers, trust me. Again, do not just expect your team to use and understand these things. Know them. Use them. You can't properly lead if the team speaks a language you don't understand. Lead from the front.

5. Test and Refine:

Implement your new systems and see how they work. Be prepared to make adjustments.

Remember, the goal here is to create a well-tuned engine with many parts working together in unison, allowing you to focus on what you do best – coaching and changing lives. Make the time to adjust now and you'll be better off later. Don't let the administrative BS hold you back from making the impact you're meant to make.

Reflection Questions:

1. What areas of your coaching business feel the most chaotic right now?

2. Which tasks do you find yourself doing over and over? How could you systematize these?

3. What's one system you could implement this week that would save you the most time?

Action Steps:

1. Choose one area of your business (e.g., client onboarding) and map out your current process.

2. Identify three tasks you do repeatedly and create SOPs for them.

3. Research and choose one tool (CRM, project management software, etc.) to help systemize your business.

Download the free printable PDF workbook with ALL the Action Steps, additional guides, templates and MORE:
http://engineforimpact.com/workbook

Chapter 5: The Automation Advantage: Enhancing Client Relationships

We've talked about systems, but now it's time to kick it up a notch. Let's talk about automation. And before you roll your eyes thinking this is some tech-bro bullshit, listen up. Automation isn't about replacing the human touch in your coaching – it's about enhancing it.

Here's the deal: Your most valuable asset as a coach is your time. Every minute you spend on mundane, repetitive tasks is a minute you're not spending on what really matters—changing your clients' lives. That's where automation comes in.

Now, I get it. When I first transitioned from the structured world of NYC consulting to fitness coaching, I was skeptical about automation. I thought it would make my approach feel impersonal, robotic even. Wow, was I wrong.

Let me explain. When done right, automation doesn't diminish your personal touch—it amplifies it. It frees you up to focus on the high-value, high-impact activities that truly make a difference to your clients.

Here's why automation is a game-changer:

1. Consistency:

Automated systems ensure no client falls through the cracks. Every touchpoint, every follow-up, happens like clockwork.

2. Scalability:

Want to grow your client base without working 24/7? Automation is your secret weapon. You can help more people and make more money. Period.

3. Personalization:

Contrary to popular belief, good automation allows for more personalization, not less. We'll get into how in a minute.

4. Client Experience:

A "well-tuned engine" kind of system creates a smooth, professional experience for your clients from day one. They won't resent it. They will appreciate it. It's professional and sets the tone for how they feel about the kind of business you're running.

So, where should you start with automation? Let's break it down:

1. Client Onboarding:

Automate your welcome sequence. Set up a series of emails that go out automatically when a new client signs up. Include all the necessary info, forms to fill out, and next steps. Make them feel welcomed and prepared from the get-go. They should be led from step to step without anyone having to lift a finger. Clear, concise guidance. Simple yet effective.

2. Appointment Scheduling:

Use tools like Calendly or Acuity to let clients book their sessions without the back-and-forth email dance. Trust me, this alone will save you hours each week.

3. Follow-ups and Check-ins:

Set up automated email sequences to check in with clients between sessions. Ask about their progress, challenges, and wins. This keeps them engaged and gives you valuable info to work with in your next session. Respond without automation once they answer the initial follow-up. You maintain a personal touch while still operating mundane tasks on autopilot.

4. Content Delivery:

Use an automated system to deliver workout plans, nutrition guides, or educational content. This ensures your clients always have the resources they need at their fingertips.

5. Payment Processing:

Automate your billing. No more chasing payments or awkward money conversations. Set it and forget it.

Now, here's where the magic happens. These automated systems? They're not just about efficiency. They're about creating space for real, meaningful interactions with your clients.

Let me give you a personal example. When I was in high-ticket fitness coaching sales, I implemented an automated follow-up system. It would send out regular check-in emails to leads and clients. But here's the kicker – just like the approach I mentioned above, I didn't just let it run on autopilot. I used the responses to these automated emails as jumping-off points for personalized outreach. I set ways to start conversations and then got notified to continue the conversations when the lead or client was ready. They felt important. The automation enhanced the personal touch.

If a lead expressed interest in a specific type of training or had a certain objection, I could tailor my next conversation to address those things head-on.

The result? The people I interacted with felt more supported than ever, and my close rates went through the roof. All because automation gave me the bandwidth to focus on what really mattered – building relationships and delivering results.

But take note here, because this is crucial: Automation is a tool, not a crutch. You can't just set it up and forget about it. You need to review and refine your automated systems regularly. Are they delivering the results you want? Are your clients responding well? Be prepared to tweak and adjust as needed.

Also, never forget the importance of the human touch. Use automation to handle the routine stuff, but always be ready to jump in personally when it matters. Your automated system should tell you when that is.

So, how do you get started with automation? Here's your game plan:

1. Map Your Client Journey:

Map out every touchpoint, from first contact to ongoing coaching. This will show you where automation can have the biggest impact.

2. Choose Your Tools:

There are tons of automation tools out there. Do your research and choose ones that integrate well with each other. I'm talking about CRMs, email marketing platforms, scheduling tools, the works. Don't necessarily just pick the recognizable brand name. Think it through.

3. Start Small:

Don't try to automate everything at once. Start with one area, like client onboarding, and build from there. One brick at a time when building a health and fitness foundation. One brick at a time when building a solid business foundation.

4. Test and Refine:

Once you've set up an automated system, test it rigorously. Put yourself in your client's shoes. Is the experience smooth and professional?

5. Keep the Human Touch:

Always include options for clients to reach out personally if they need to. Make sure your automated communications sound like you, not some corporate robot.

Remember, the goal of automation is to enhance your coaching, not replace it. Use it to create space for more meaningful interactions, more personalized guidance, and, ultimately, better results for your clients.

Reflection Questions:

1. What repetitive tasks are currently eating up most of your time?

2. Where in your client journey do you see opportunities for automation?

3. What aspects of your coaching do you want to ensure always have a personal touch?

Action Steps:

1. Choose one area of your business to automate this week. It could be appointment scheduling or client check-ins.

2. Research and select an automation tool that fits your needs.

3. Test a simple automated sequence (like a welcome email series) thoroughly.

Download the free printable PDF workbook with ALL the Action Steps, additional guides, templates and MORE:

http://engineforimpact.com/workbook

Chapter 6: Mastering Content Batching for Consistent Marketing

Let's talk about something that's probably driving you crazy right now: content creation. As someone who's transitioned from sales to coaching, I get it. Content creation wasn't part of my daily grind when I was in sales, but I quickly realized its importance in the coaching world.

Here's the truth: Content is your lifeline as a coach in today's digital landscape. It's how you attract new clients, nurture leads, and keep the current clients engaged. But here's the kicker – you can't let content creation take over your life. That's where content batching comes in.

Now, I know what you're thinking. "Great, another thing to add to my to-do list." But stick with me here. Content batching isn't about doing more; it's about working smarter. It's about creating a system (remember what we said about systems?) that allows you to produce high-quality content consistently without losing your mind.

When I first started considering the move to coaching, I saw many coaches struggling with content creation. They were either posting sporadically, posting generic stuff, or burning out, trying to create daily content. None of this was effective.

Here's why content batching is a game-changer:

1. Efficiency:

When you batch your content, you get into a flow state. You're not constantly switching gears, producing more in less time.

2. Consistency:

With a backlog of content, you'll never miss a post because you're too busy or don't feel inspired.

3. Quality:

When you're not rushing to create content at the last minute, you have time to refine and improve your message.

4. Strategy:

Batching lets you plan your content strategically, ensuring it aligns with your business goals and client needs.

So, how do you make this work? Let's break it down:

1. Set Aside Dedicated Time:

Block out several hours, or even a full day, solely for content creation. Treat this time like you would a client session – it's non-negotiable.

2. Plan Your Content in Advance:

Before your batching session, plan out your topics. Use a content calendar to align your content with your business goals and any upcoming promotions.

3. Create Templates:

Develop templates for different types of content – blog posts, social media captions, email newsletters. This gives you a starting point and ensures consistency in your messaging.

4. Batch Similar Tasks:

Group similar tasks together. Write all your blog posts at once, then move on to creating social media graphics, and then record all your videos. This keeps you in the zone.

5. Use Tools to Your Advantage:

Leverage tools like Canva for graphics, Hootsuite for scheduling social media posts, and Trello for organizing content ideas.

6. Repurpose Content:

Don't reinvent the wheel every time. A single piece of content can be repurposed into multiple formats. That blog post? Turn it into a series of social media posts, a video script, and an email newsletter. A livestream or webinar? Pop it into Opus Clip and get a week's worth of reels. The game has changed. One piece of information can be repackaged a million ways and hit a million people without seeming stale. It's about balance and planning.

As I mentioned, I didn't create content as a salesperson, but I saw firsthand how powerful consistent communication was in nurturing leads and closing deals. The principles are the same—it's about staying top-of-mind and consistently providing value. I've incorporated these concepts recently, and the benefits are visible immediately.

But listen up – content batching isn't about creating a ton of generic, one-size-fits-all content. It's about efficiently creating personalized, valuable content that resonates with your audience. Remember, authenticity is key. Your batched content should sound like you, address your client's real needs, and provide genuine value.

Here's how to get started:

1. Identify Your Content Needs:

What types of content will best serve your audience and your business goals? Blog posts? Social media content? Email newsletters? Track your metrics. Make data-informed decisions (which we discuss in the next chapter).

2. Create a Content Calendar:

Map out your content for the next month or quarter. Align it with your business goals and client needs.

3. Set Up Your Batching System:

Choose your tools, create your templates, and schedule your first batching session.

4. Start Small:

Don't try to batch a year's worth of content in one go. Start with a week or two and build from there.

5. Review and Refine:

After implementing your batching system, review its effectiveness. Are you saving time? Is your content quality improving? Adjust as needed.

Remember, content batching aims to free up your time and mental energy so you can focus on what matters – coaching your clients and growing your business. It's about working smarter, not harder.

Content creation might be new territory for you, but with smart batching, you can create a consistent, high-quality content stream that attracts clients and builds your authority – all while freeing up your time to do what you do best. Are you ready to become a content creation machine? Let's make it happen.

Reflection Questions:

1. What types of content do you think would be most valuable for your target audience?

2. How could you realistically implement content batching in your current schedule?

3. What skills from your life experiences could you leverage in your content creation?

Action Steps:

1. Create a content calendar for the next month.

2. Schedule your first content batching session.

3. Develop one template for a social media post, a blog post, and an email newsletter.

Download the free printable PDF workbook with ALL the Action Steps, additional guides, templates and MORE:
http://engineforimpact.com/workbook

Chapter 7: Leveraging Data for Strategic Decision-Making

Next step, coach. It's time to talk about something that might make your eyes glaze over, but trust me, it's crucial: data. Now, I know what you're thinking. "I became a coach to help people, not to crunch numbers." But here's the deal: in today's digital world, data is your secret weapon for growing your business and serving your clients better.

I'm sure you tell your clients to track their macros or record *something* in their daily lives. Track steps? Habits? Reps? Food? Weight? No matter which niche of the health and fitness coaching industry, you're telling your clients to record information and make data-driven decisions to optimize their journey from "Point A" to "Point B" as fast and efficiently as possible. Think of all of your business data like that. The data from marketing, sales, and social media are all macros. You can see how to adjust and make things work better. Don't think you're above it. You're not.

When I transitioned from the structured world of NYC consulting to the fitness industry, I was shocked at how many coaches were living in a blindspot when it came to their measurable metrics. They were making decisions based on gut feelings and random observations or they were flat out just copying other coaches that were more successful. That might work for a while, but if you want to build a sustainable, scalable coaching business, you need to get serious about data.

Here's why data matters:

1. Clarity:

Data cuts through the bullshit. It shows you exactly what's working and not in your business.

2. Efficiency:

By understanding your numbers, you can focus your time and energy on the activities that actually move the needle.

3. Growth:

Data helps you identify trends and opportunities you might otherwise miss.

4. Client Results:

By tracking the right metrics, you can improve your coaching and get better client results.

So, what data should you be tracking? Let's break it down:

1. Client Acquisition:

- Lead sources: Where are your clients coming from?

- Conversion rates: How many leads turn into paying clients?
- Cost per acquisition: How much are you spending to get each new client?

2. Client Retention:

- Churn rate: How many clients are you losing each month?
- Lifetime value: How much does each client spend with you over time?
- Engagement metrics: How often are clients interacting with your content or services?

3. Financial Health:

- Revenue: Obviously, you need to know how much you're bringing in.
- Profit margins: It's not just about revenue - are you actually making money?
- Cash flow: Are you managing your money effectively month to month?

4. Client Results:

- Success metrics: Are your clients achieving their goals?
- Satisfaction scores: How happy are your clients with your services?

5. Marketing Effectiveness:

- Content engagement: Which of your content pieces are resonating most?
- Email open and click rates: Are your emails actually being read?
- Social media metrics: Which platforms and post types are driving the most engagement?

This may seem overwhelming. But remember, you don't need to track everything at once. Start with the metrics that most closely align with your current business goals. Brick by brick. Day by day. Stack the little wins. One at a time.

Here's a personal example: I obsessively tracked my lead sources and conversion rates when I was in high-ticket fitness coaching sales. By doing this, I quickly realized that leads from referrals converted at a much higher rate than those from cold outreach. This data led me to shift my strategy, focusing more on cultivating referrals. The result? My close rates improved dramatically, and my income grew as a result.

But here's the thing - and pay attention because this is crucial - data is useless if you don't act on it. It's not enough to collect numbers. You need to analyze them, draw insights, and make decisions based on what you're learning from those numbers.

So, how do you get started with data-driven decision-making?

Here's your game plan:

1. Identify Your Key Metrics:

Choose 3-5 metrics that are most important for your business as it is currently. Don't overwhelm yourself with too many numbers too soon.

2. Set Up Tracking Systems:

Use tools like Google Analytics for your website, built-in analytics for your social media, and your CRM for client data. Make sure you have a system to collect and organize this data regularly. Down the line, see if you can integrate all of these separate sources into one main comprehensive dashboard.

3. Schedule Regular Review Sessions:

Set aside time each week or month to review your data. Look for trends, anomalies, and areas for improvement.

4. Make Data-Informed Decisions:

Use your insights to make concrete changes in your business.

Test new strategies based on the data.

5. Iterate and Improve:

Continuously refine your approach based on the results you're seeing. Data-driven decision-making is an ongoing process.

Remember, the goal here isn't to become a data scientist. It's to use data as a tool to build a more successful, impactful coaching business. You're still a coach first - data is just there to support and enhance your coaching.

Reflection Questions:

1. What metrics are you currently tracking in your business? Are they giving you the insights you need?

2. Where do you feel you're making decisions blindly in your business? How could data help?

3. What's one area of your business where better data could lead to immediate improvements?

Action Steps:

1. Choose your top 3 key performance indicators (KPIs) to start tracking.

2. Set up a simple spreadsheet or choose a tool to track these KPIs (We have some free templates in our free Facebook Community. Link is at the end of the book or on our website. Engineforimpact.com)

3. Schedule a weekly 30-minute session to review your data and draw insights.

Download the free printable PDF workbook with ALL the Action Steps, additional guides, templates and MORE:

http://engineforimpact.com/workbook

Chapter 8: The Art of Virtual Group Coaching

Part 1: Getting Started with Virtual Group Coaching

If you're not doing virtual group coaching yet, listen up. You're leaving money on the table and limiting your impact (if you already are, skip to "Part 2" of this chapter). I get it - you like the personal touch of one-on-one coaching. But here's the truth: group coaching isn't about watering down your service. It's about scaling your impact and your income.

When I transitioned from high-ticket sales to business coaching, I quickly realized that one-on-one coaching alone wouldn't be enough to build a sustainable, scalable business. Virtual group coaching was the game-changer. Getting the conversation in front of more people able to share different views and ask different questions expands the value of what you're putting out there. More minds will always be better than one.

Here's why you need to add virtual group coaching to your arsenal:

1. Scalability:
Serve more clients in less time. Simple math.

2. Community Building:
Groups create a sense of belonging and accountability among clients.

3. Diverse Perspectives:
Clients learn not just from you but also from each other.

4. Increased Value:

Often, clients get more value from group coaching than they would one-on-one. Instead of just once a week 1 on 1 meetings, they can have access to multiple hour long conversations.

5. Profit Margins:
Higher profit potential with less time investment.

But here's the kicker - running a successful virtual group coaching program isn't just about throwing a bunch of people into a Zoom call. It's an art form.

Here's how to master it:

1. Define Your Niche:

Your group program should solve a specific problem for a specific type of person. The more focused, the better.

2. Structure Your Program:

Have a clear curriculum and timeline. People need to know what they're getting and when.

3. Foster Community:

Use platforms like Facebook groups or Slack channels to keep the conversation going in between sessions.

4. Master Group Facilitation:

Learn how to manage group dynamics, ensure everyone participates, and handle difficult personalities.

5. Leverage Technology:

Use tools that enhance the group experience. Think interactive whiteboards, polling features, and breakout rooms.

6. Provide Individual Attention:

Find ways to give personal feedback within the group setting. This could be hot seats, written feedback, or short one-on-one check-ins.

7. Create Accountability:

Set up systems for participants to track their progress and hold each other accountable.

Let me be clear: virtual group coaching isn't about providing less value. It's about providing value differently. When done right, your clients can get even better results than they would one-on-one.

Here's a personal insight: I saw how powerful group dynamics could be in driving results in the high-ticket fitness world. The camaraderie, the friendly competition, the shared victories - these elements often pushed clients further than they'd go alone. They felt ingrained in a "society" of like-minded, driven people. They felt pushed to make sure they didn't let the team down. This led to an intrinsic level of motivation they wouldn't necessarily find by doing it alone or just with 1 on 1 conversation with their coach.

But listen up because this is crucial: the success of your group program hinges on your ability to create a powerful group experience. You need to be part coach, part facilitator, part community manager.

So, how do you get started with virtual group coaching? Here's your game plan:

1. Identify Your Offer:

What problem will your group program solve? Who is it for? What's the desired outcome?

2. Design Your Program:

Map out your curriculum. What will you cover each week? Is there prerecorded coursework? Rotating topics? Topics assigned to specific days and time slots? What exercises or assignments will participants do?

3. Choose Your Technology:

Select your video conferencing platform, community management tool, and other tech necessary to maximize your impact.

4. Set Your Pricing:

Price your program based on the value provided, not just the time spent. Remember, this is about scale.

5. Create Your Marketing Plan:

How will you fill your group program? Will you market to your existing audience, run ads, or both?

6. Pilot Your Program:

Start with a small group to test and refine your approach before scaling up.

Remember, transitioning to group coaching doesn't mean abandoning one-on-one work entirely. Many successful coaches offer a mix of both, using group programs to serve more people and as a pipeline for high-ticket one-on-one clients.

Reflection Questions:

1. What aspects of your one-on-one coaching could translate well to a group setting?

2. What concerns do you have about moving into group coaching, and how could you address them?

3. What unique value could you offer in a group program that differs from your one-on-one coaching?

Action Steps:

1. Outline a potential 6-week group coaching program in your niche.

2. Research and choose one platform for hosting your virtual group sessions.

3. Identify 5-10 current or past clients who might be interested in a group program and ask them for feedback on your idea.

Download the free printable PDF workbook with ALL the Action Steps, additional guides, templates and MORE:

http://engineforimpact.com/workbook

Part 2: Elevating Your Virtual Group Coaching Game

You've already taken the leap into virtual group coaching, which is good for you. But here's the thing: in this fast-paced digital world, what worked yesterday might not cut it tomorrow. It's time to level up your group coaching game.

In high-ticket fitness coaching, I saw plenty of coaches running group programs. But the ones who really killed it? They were constantly innovating, refining, and pushing the boundaries of what group coaching could be. Let's make sure you're in that category.

Here are the key areas where you can take your virtual group coaching from good to great:

1. Personalization at Scale:

Just because it's a group doesn't mean it can't feel personal. Use data and technology to tailor the experience for each participant. Think personalized action plans, AI-powered recommendations, or custom content paths based on individual progress.

2. Interactive Content:

Static presentations are out, and interactive content is in. Use tools like Mentimeter for live polls, Miro for collaborative brainstorming, or Kahoot for gamified learning to keep your participants engaged and active throughout each session.

3. Micro-Learning Modules:

Break your content into bite-sized, actionable pieces. This isn't just about shorter attention spans - it's about making your content easy to implement. Create 5-minute daily challenges or short video lessons to complement your main sessions.

4. Peer-to-Peer Learning:

Leverage your group's collective wisdom. Set up peer coaching sessions, create accountability partnerships, or use a platform like Slack for ongoing peer discussions. Remember, in a great group program, participants learn as much from each other as they do from you.

5. Multimodal Learning:

People learn differently. Offer your content in various formats - video, audio, text, and interactive exercises. This isn't more work for you; it's about repurposing your content to cater to different learning styles.

6. Advanced Analytics:

Go beyond basic attendance and satisfaction metrics. Track individual and group progress, engagement levels, and content interaction rates. Use this data to continuously refine your program and provide more targeted support.

7. High-Touch/Low-Touch Balance:

Find the sweet spot between personal attention and scalability. Could you offer tiered programs? A base level with group sessions only, and premium tiers with added 1:1 support or VIP level masterminds?

8. Community Building 2.0:

Don't just create a community - cultivate it. Appoint community leaders from your star participants. Create challenges that foster connection. Use tools like Mighty Networks to create a branded community experience.

9. Continuous Feedback Loop:

Regular surveys are good, but real-time feedback is better. Use tools like Hotjar to understand how participants interact with your online materials. Implement live feedback features in your sessions. Make adjusting your program on the fly part of your process.

10. Ascension Model:

Your group program shouldn't be the end of the line. How can it feed into higher-ticket offerings? Could top performers from your group program be invited to an exclusive mastermind? Or offered one-on-one coaching packages?

Now, here's a personal insight: In the high-ticket fitness world, I saw how the most successful programs were those that created genuine transformation. They weren't just delivering content—they were changing lives. And that's what you need to aim for.

But listen up because this is crucial: Innovation for innovation's sake is pointless. Every change you make should serve your clients better and move them more effectively towards their goals. Always ask, "How does this improve the client experience and results?"

So, how do you implement these upgrades? Here's your game plan:

1. Audit Your Current Program:

What's working well? Where are people dropping off or disengaging? Use data and participant feedback to identify areas for improvement.

2. Prioritize Improvements:

You can't change everything at once. Pick the 2-3 areas that will have the biggest impact and focus on those first.

3. Test and Iterate:

Don't wait for perfection. Implement changes in small batches, gather feedback, and refine as you go. Fail. Fix. Fail. Fix. Succeed.

4. Upskill Yourself:

Invest in your own learning. Whether it's group facilitation skills, the latest in higher-level mentorship opportunities (Hit me up, I know a guy), or advanced coaching methodologies - stay at the cutting edge.

5. Leverage Technology:

Research and invest in tools that can help you deliver a more engaging, personalized, and effective group experience.

Remember, the goal isn't just to have a good group program. It's to have the best damn group program in your niche. One that gets results, creates raving fans, and positions you as the go-to expert in your field. The world of virtual group coaching is evolving rapidly. It's not enough just to keep up - you must strive to lead the pack. Are you ready to take your group coaching to the next level and deliver an experience your clients can't get anywhere else?

Reflection Questions:

1. What's the biggest complaint or point of friction in your current group program? How could you address it?

2. How could you make your program more engaging and interactive?

3. What additional value could you offer that would make your program irresistible to potential clients?

Action Steps:

1. Implement one new interactive element in your next group session. Get feedback from clients.

2. Set up a system to track at least three new metrics about your program's effectiveness.

3. Create a survey for current and past participants to gather in-depth feedback on your program.

Download the free printable PDF workbook with ALL the Action Steps, additional guides, templates and MORE:
http://engineforimpact.com/workbook

Chapter 9: Customizing CRM Systems for Optimal Client Management

We're about to dive into something that might not get people very fired up, but it's absolutely crucial for scaling your business: Customer Relationship Management (CRM) systems. If you're still managing your clients with spreadsheets or, God forbid, pen and paper, you're not just behind the times – you're actively sabotaging your growth.

Now, I've always used CRMs, from my days in high-ticket sales to my transition into the coaching world. And let me tell you, the power of a well-customized CRM in the coaching business is unmatched. It's not just about tracking sales or storing contact info – it's about creating a central nervous system for your entire coaching operation.

Here's why a well-customized CRM is non-negotiable:

1. Centralized Information:

All your client data in one place. No more digging through emails or notebooks.

2. Automated Follow-ups:

Never let a lead or client fall through the cracks again.

3. Performance Tracking:

Monitor client progress and your business metrics in real-time.

4. Time Saving:

Automate repetitive tasks and free up your time for high-value activities.

5. Scalability:

Manage more clients without drowning in admin work.

But here's the kicker – it's not enough to just sign up for a CRM and call it a day. The power is in the customization. You need to tailor your CRM to fit your specific coaching business like a glove.

Let's break down how to customize your CRM for maximum impact:

1. Define Your Client Journey:

Map out every touchpoint from lead to long-term client. Your CRM should reflect this journey. Do not just use this system for the sales process and abandon it. It should connect you to your clients and their information every step of the way. From the first sales call until they reach their goals and no longer need your services.

2. Identify Key Data Points:

What information do you need to track for each client? Goals, progress metrics, communication preferences – get granular. See if you can integrate any other tracking software right into your CRM. A "master" hub for everything is ideal.

3. Set Up Custom Fields:

Most higher-level CRMs allow you to create custom fields. Use these to track coaching-specific information that generic CRMs might not cover.

4. Create Automated Workflows:

Set up sequences for onboarding, check-ins, and follow-ups. The more you can automate, the more you can scale.

5. Integrate with Other Tools:

Connect your CRM with your email marketing platform, scheduling tool, and payment processor for a seamless system.

6. Customize Reporting:

Set up dashboards that give you at-a-glance insights into your business health and client progress.

7. Train Your Team:

If you have a team, make sure everyone knows how to use the CRM effectively. Consistency is key. SOPs and thorough onboarding with video tutorials are crucial. The team shouldn't be figuring it out as they go. They shouldn't have some hack job training either. This should be as calculated as one of your coaching programs. You really have 2 different groups of people to lead and coach if you're doing it right.

Now, let me share a personal insight. When I was in high-ticket fitness coaching sales, we used a CRM. It was, unfortunately, just for tracking sales – it could've been used to monitor client progress, automate check-ins, and even predict which clients might be at risk of dropping off. This level of insight would have been invaluable for providing top-notch service and hitting our retention targets.

Pay attention, because this is crucial: Your CRM is only as good as the data you put into it and how consistently you use it. It needs to become an integral part of your daily workflow, not just another tool you check occasionally.

So, how do you get started with customizing your CRM? Here's your game plan:

1. Choose the Right CRM:

Research options that could cater to coaches or have high customizability. Popular choices include HubSpot, Pipedrive, HighLevel, or coaching-specific options like TrueCoach. Check the integration options. Make sure you can tie things together seamlessly wherever possible.

2. Start with the Basics:

Begin with essential features like contact management and task tracking. Get comfortable with these before diving into more advanced customizations.

3. Map Your Processes:

Document your client acquisition, onboarding, and coaching processes. Use this as a blueprint for setting up your CRM. Create and adjust your pipelines to fit your specific business needs.

4. Implement in Phases:

Don't try to do everything at once. Start with one area of your business, perfect it, then move on to the next.

5. Regular Reviews:

Schedule monthly reviews to assess how well your CRM is working and what needs tweaking.

The goal isn't just to have a CRM. It's to have a centralized system that makes your coaching business run like a well-oiled machine, freeing you up to focus on what you do best – coaching.

Reflection Questions:

1. What parts of your client management process are currently the most time-consuming or prone to error?

2. What key metrics do you wish you had easy access to in your business?

3. How could better client data management improve your coaching outcomes?

Action Steps:

1. Research and choose a CRM that fits your business needs or optimize the system you are currently using through adjustments and/or integrations to your other software systems.

2. List out all the data points you want to track for each client.

3. Set up one automated workflow in your CRM, such as a client onboarding sequence.

Download the free printable PDF workbook with ALL the Action Steps, additional guides, templates and MORE:
http://engineforimpact.com/workbook

Chapter 10: Strategic Outsourcing: Focusing on Your Core Competencies

Alright, coach. It's time to talk about something that separates the amateurs from the pros in this business: strategic outsourcing. If you're still trying to do everything yourself, you're not just limiting your growth – you're probably delivering a subpar experience to your clients.

I've seen this firsthand. In my consulting days, I watched businesses crumble under the weight of trying to do it all. And in the fitness industry? Same story, different setting. The coaches who truly scaled were the ones who mastered the art of delegation.

Here's the truth: You can't be world-class at everything. And you shouldn't try to be. Your time and energy are finite resources. Every minute you spend on tasks that aren't in your zone of genius is a minute you're not spending on what truly moves the needle in your business.

So, let's break down why strategic outsourcing is crucial:

1. Focus:

It allows you to concentrate on what you do best – coaching and growing your business.

2. Expertise:

You get access to specialized skills without the overhead of full-time employees.

3. Scalability:

You can grow your business without proportionally increasing your workload.

4. Quality:

Tasks get done by people who specialize in them, often resulting in better outcomes.

5. Time:

You reclaim hours in your day for high-value activities or, dare I say it, some actual work-life balance.

Now, I know what some of you are thinking. "But I can't afford to outsource." Let me stop you right there. You can't afford *not* to outsource. It's an investment in your business and your sanity.

Here's how to approach outsourcing strategically:

1. Identify Your Core Competencies:

What are you truly the best at? What activities drive the most value in your business? These are the things you should never outsource.

2. Audit Your Time:

Track how you spend your time for a week. I bet you'll be shocked at how much is spent on low-value tasks.

3. Prioritize Outsourcing Opportunities:

Look for repetitive tasks, specialized skills you lack, and time-consuming activities that don't directly generate revenue.

4. Start Small:

You don't have to outsource everything at once. Start with one or two tasks and build from there.

5. Hire for Outcomes, Not Hours:

Focus on what you want accomplished, not on micromanaging someone's time.

6. Develop Systems and Processes:

Document your workflows before outsourcing. This ensures consistency and makes it easier to delegate.

7. Invest in Relationships:

Whether you're hiring freelancers or agencies, treat them as partners in your business, not just service providers.

Now, let me share a personal insight. In fitness coaching sales, I saw many coaches burn out trying to handle everything themselves. The ones who succeeded focused on their strengths—motivating clients, designing programs, and creating content—and outsourced the rest.

This is crucial: Outsourcing isn't about abdicating responsibility. You're still the captain of the ship. You must set clear expectations, communicate effectively, and manage your outsourced team.

So, what should you consider outsourcing? Here's a starter list:

1. Administrative Tasks:

Scheduling, data entry, email management.

2. Content Creation:

Blog posts, some social media content (you need to be involved in a good amount of this), email newsletters.

3. Design Work:

Graphics, website design, marketing materials.

4. Tech Support:

Website maintenance, app development, systems integration.

5. Bookkeeping and Accounting:

Financial record-keeping, tax prep.

6. Customer Support:

Handling basic client inquiries and managing your inbox.

Remember, the goal is to free you up to focus on the activities that truly require your unique skills and drive the most value in your business. Strategic outsourcing isn't just about offloading work – it's about optimizing your business for growth and impact. It's about working smarter, not harder. Are you ready to focus on what you do best and let experts handle the rest?

Reflection Questions:

1. What tasks currently consume most of your time but don't directly contribute to growth or client outcomes?

2. What skills do you lack that, if you had them, would significantly improve your business?

3. What's holding you back from outsourcing? Fear, budget, control issues?

Action Steps:

1. Identify three tasks you currently do that could be outsourced.

2. Research platforms like Upwork or Fiverr to understand the market rates for these tasks.

3. Create a detailed process document for one task you're ready to outsource.

Download the free printable PDF workbook with ALL the Action Steps, additional guides, templates and MORE:
http://engineforimpact.com/workbook

Chapter 11:Self-Care Practices for Coaches: Avoiding Burnout

We need to have a serious talk about something that could make or break your business and your life: self-care. I know, I know. You're probably rolling your eyes thinking, "I don't have time for this fluffy stuff. I need to go hard *all the time* to level up." But let me tell you, ignoring self-care isn't just stupid – it's downright dangerous for your business.

I've seen it firsthand. In the high-pressure world of NYC consulting and later in high-ticket fitness coaching, I watched talented professionals flame out because they neglected their own well-being. Don't be that person.

Here's the cold, hard truth: You can't pour from an empty cup. If you're burnt out, stressed out, and run down, you're not just hurting yourself – you're shortchanging your clients and sabotaging your business.

So let's break down why self-care isn't just important – it's non-negotiable:

1. Sustainability:

This is a marathon, not a sprint. Self-care ensures you can keep performing at a high-level long-term.

2. Creativity:

A fresh, rested mind is more innovative and better at problem-solving.

3. Empathy:

When you're taken care of, you have more emotional bandwidth for your clients.

4. Modeling:

You're in the business of health and wellness. Practice what you preach.

5. Decision Making:

Stress and burnout lead to poor choices. Self-care keeps you sharp.

Self-care isn't just about bubble baths and meditation apps (though if that's your thing, go for it). It's about creating sustainable practices that keep you at the top of your game.

Here's how to approach it:

1. Set Boundaries:

Learn to say no. Set office hours and stick to them. Your clients will respect you more for it.

2. Prioritize Sleep:

Seriously. Nothing else matters if you're not getting enough quality sleep.

3. Move Your Body:

You're a health and/or fitness coach for crying out loud. Make time for your own workouts.

4. Fuel Properly:

Eat like you tell your clients to eat. Your body and brain need premium fuel.

5. Schedule Downtime:

Put it in your calendar like any other important appointment because it is.

6. Continuous Learning:

Invest in your personal and professional development. It keeps you engaged and growing.

7. Build a Support Network:

Surround yourself with people who get it. Fellow coaches, mentors, and friends who support your goals.

8. Regular Check-ins:

Schedule time to assess your stress levels and overall well-being. Catch issues before they become problems.

Here's a personal insight: When I was grinding in high-ticket sales, there was a point where I didn't prioritize time for self-care. I would often find myself working longer hours than I should've been. Know where that got me? Nowhere good. It wasn't until I started prioritizing my well-being that I saw my performance bounce back. It can feel counterintuitive when you're trying to grind, but you need to force yourself.

Now listen up because this is crucial: Self-care isn't selfish. It's a business strategy. When you're operating at your best, everyone wins – you, your clients, and your bottom line.

So, how do you implement a solid self-care routine? Here's your game plan:

1. Audit Your Current Habits:

Be honest about where you're falling short in taking care of yourself.

2. Identify Your Non-Negotiables:

What are the bare minimum self-care practices you need to function well? Start there.

3. Schedule It:

One more time, put self-care activities on your calendar. Treat them with the same respect you'd give to a client appointment.

4. Start Small:

Don't try to overhaul your entire life overnight. Pick one or two areas to focus on and build from there. I'm sure this is what you tell your clients, follow your own advice.

5. Accountability:

Share your self-care goals with someone who'll hold you to them. Maybe even a fellow coach.

Self-care isn't a luxury but necessary for any coach who wants to build a sustainable, thriving business. It's about playing the long game. Are you ready to invest in your most important asset – yourself?

Reflection Questions:

1. What areas of self-care are you currently neglecting?

2. How is your current level of self-care affecting your coaching performance?

3. What's one self-care practice you could implement this week that would have the biggest impact?

Action Steps:

1. Schedule three 30-minute blocks of "me time" in your calendar for next week.

2. Identify one boundary you must set and communicate it to your clients or team.

3. Start a daily practice of checking in with yourself. How are you feeling? What do you need?

Download the free printable PDF workbook with ALL the Action Steps, additional guides, templates and MORE:
http://engineforimpact.com/workbook

Chapter 12: Continuous Learning: Staying Ahead in a Dynamic Industry

In the fast-paced world of high-ticket fitness sales and marketing, complacency is the kiss of death. I learned this lesson quickly when I transitioned from the structured environment of consulting to the ever-evolving landscape of fitness industry sales.

At first, I thought my background in consulting had prepared me for anything. I had my pitch down pat, my objection handlers memorized, and a solid grasp of the fitness programs we were selling. But I soon realized that wasn't enough. The fitness industry moves at lightning speed, constantly emerging new trends, research, and consumer preferences.

I remember sitting in on a sales call with a potential client who started asking about a new training methodology I'd never heard of. I fumbled through the call to steer the conversation back to familiar territory. After hanging up, I knew I had lost that sale – and possibly future referrals – because I wasn't up to date. It completely destroyed my credibility during that conversation. It didn't feel awesome.

That day was a wake-up call. I understand that in this industry, the moment you think you know it all is when you actually know nothing (don't go full Jon Snow). It's not just about knowing your product; it's about understanding the fitness landscape, consumer psychology, and emerging trends with the actual health and fitness coaching and the business side. Don't want to use AI or automation? Your loss, your competition will be. Don't want to assess your bottlenecks and adjust? The other guys will.

Since then, I have overhauled my approach to learning. Instead of relying solely on company-provided materials, I studied fitness industry publications, psychology journals, and marketing strategy books. I set aside time each week specifically for learning—early mornings with a cup of coffee became my "self-study" sessions.

One particular book on behavioral economics led me to redesign my entire sales approach, resulting in a significantly better approach to my calls with potential clients. Who would have thought that concepts from financial decision-making could be so relevant to selling fitness programs?

But my learning journey wasn't always smooth sailing. I remember feeling overwhelmed at times by the sheer volume of information available. It was during one of these moments of information overload that I received advice from a senior colleague that changed everything.

"Don't just learn," he told me. "Apply and teach."

So, I started sharing what I was learning—with my team, in our sales meetings, even creating extensive Google Docs with industry insights. I shared my findings with the rest of the sales team. The act of sharing these things forced me to distill complex ideas into simple, actionable concepts. It not only solidified my understanding but also helped me discover which new ideas most applied to what we were trying to do.

As I continued on this path of continuous learning, I noticed a shift in my performance. My sales numbers were improving. There were still bad weeks and good weeks, but I became more consistent in my ability to adapt to each individual call. I was able to handle a wider variety of client questions and objections. Perhaps most importantly, I was more engaged and excited about my work than ever before.

But here's the thing about continuous learning in our industry – it's not just about personal growth or even sales numbers. It's about responsibility. As health and fitness industry representatives, we have a duty to our clients to stay informed and provide accurate, up-to-date information. Every new thing we learn has the potential to impact someone's health journey positively.

You aren't being paid to give them information. You are being paid to filter out the bullshit and give them the *right* information just like I am doing here for you. Just like I do for my clients when they invest in my business coaching.

This approach to continuous learning didn't just improve my sales performance; it changed my career trajectory. It gave me the knowledge and confidence to move beyond sales and into marketing strategy, where understanding industry trends and consumer behavior is paramount.

The lesson is clear: in the dynamic world of this industry's sales and marketing, your ability to learn, adapt, and evolve isn't just a nice-to-have – it's the key to your long-term success and impact. Stay curious, question your assumptions, seek new perspectives, and most importantly, apply what you learn. Because in this industry, you're falling behind if you're not constantly growing.

Reflection Questions:

1. How has your approach to learning evolved since you started your coaching business? What's working well, and what needs improvement?

2. Think about a time when you fell behind on industry trends. How did it impact your business? What did you learn from that experience?

3. In what areas of your coaching business do you feel you need to expand your knowledge most urgently? Why?

4. How do you currently balance time spent on learning with time spent on other aspects of your business? Is this balance serving you well?

5. What's your biggest obstacle to continuous learning? How can you overcome it?

Action Steps:

1. Create a learning plan for the next 90 days. Include at least one book to read, one course to take, and one industry event to attend (virtually or in-person).

2. Set up a system to stay updated on industry news. This could be subscribing to relevant newsletters, following key influencers on social media, or setting up Google Alerts for specific topics.

3. Identify a skill you want to develop that's outside your comfort zone but relevant to your business (e.g., data analysis, public speaking, content creation). Find a resource to start learning this skill and commit to spending 30 minutes a day on it for the next week.

4. Reach out to a peer or mentor in the industry to set up a knowledge-sharing session. Come prepared with specific questions or topics you want to discuss.

5. Audit your current services and programs. Identify one area where you can incorporate new industry knowledge or trends to enhance value for your clients.

Chapter 13: Leadership - Building an Empire, Not a Prison

Ok, coach. You've mastered the art of transforming bodies and minds, but now it's time to transform your business. And that starts with you stepping up as a leader—not just any leader—one who builds empires, not prisons.

Leadership isn't about barking orders or being the loudest voice in the room. It's about creating an environment where your team can thrive, innovate, and drive your business into sustainable future success. But here's the kicker: most executives, business owners, and coaches get this dead wrong. I've seen it happen in every career path I've been on.

Let's discuss the leadership spectrum. On one end, you have the dictator—the "my way or the highway" type. The "stay in your lane" type. On the other hand, you have a democratic leader who values input and collaboration. Where do you fall?

If you're leaning towards dictatorship, thinking it's the fast track to success, I have news: you're sprinting towards failure. You might feel in control and get early results, but you're suffocating the people who could take your business to the next level. You will limit the speed you can scale as you end up with a high staff turnover rate. Constantly training new people stifles growth. You're a dictator? People will quit as soon as they find something better. They also will not be giving their daily work everything they've got. You'll end up with a combination of people doing the bare minimum with one foot out the door and new hires. Does that sound like a recipe for success and growth? No, it sounds like a recipe to hit a plateau when trying to scale.

I've seen it time and time again. Business owners who think they know it all, who shut down ideas that aren't their own, who create a culture of fear rather than innovation. They might see short-term gains, but long-term? They're building a house of cards that'll collapse at the first sign of trouble.

Now, let's flip the script. Imagine a business where ideas flow freely, your team feels empowered to make decisions, and innovation isn't just encouraged—it's expected. That's what happens when you embrace a more democratic leadership style.

But don't get it twisted. Being a democratic leader doesn't mean being a pushover. It means being smart enough to realize that the collective intelligence of your team is your greatest asset. It means creating an environment where people aren't afraid to speak up, where diversity of thought is valued, and where the best ideas win - regardless of where they come from. Also, celebrate your team members when you incorporate their ideas. Don't take credit. Give credit where credit is due.

Now, let's talk about motivation. If you still rely on the carrot-and-stick approach, you live in the past. External motivation—rewards and punishments—might get short-term results, but intrinsic motivation will drive your business forward in the long run. You can still reward your team for a job well done, but this shouldn't be the only way you operate.

So, how do you light that fire from within? It starts with meaningful work. Your team needs to know that what they're doing matters. They're not just crunching numbers or sending emails - they're changing lives. Every task and every project should be connected to your larger mission. Make them see that they're not just employees, they are your team - they're empire builders.

When I say they are your "team," that means you should always make them feel that way. Little words can go a long way. If you aren't already doing so, try to refer to your staff as your "team" instead of things like "employee," or "staff." Don't say "someone that works for me". Say they "work *with* you." Aiming to create the feeling of inclusion in something bigger than oneself will add up over time. You will create a subconscious desire not to let the team down.

People don't often worry about letting their *boss* down. They don't want to *upset* their boss. They don't want the hellfire that comes with that. Not letting down the *team* hits differently psychologically. You will get out what you put in here. You can be the president of this democracy and still make the final veto or issue an executive order, but when your people feel like part of a team? Sky's the limit on what they are willing to do to help you grow. A team's mission will mean more to them than *your* personal goals. Every time.

Next up: autonomy. Nothing kills motivation faster than a boss breathing down your neck and questioning every decision. Micromanagement is the enemy of scalability. Set clear expectations, provide the resources your team needs, and get out of their way. You might be surprised at what they can achieve when given the freedom to own their work. You actually want people to make minor mistakes. This leads to growth in the long run. Hovering will create a state of "second-guessing." You want decision makers. An army of confident people that are constantly pushing things forward.

But freedom without growth is like a workout without progression—pointless. Your team craves mastery just as much as your clients crave results. Invest in their skills and provide opportunities for learning and development. It's not an expense—it's an investment in your empire's future.

The team I was employed with invested in a sales coach for us. It was game changing. Were we "bad" at our jobs? Not at all. We were being given additional tools for growth. It didn't feel like an attack. It felt like there was a common goal to all perform better. We learned a lot from the sales coach and we were able to create more opportunities for ourselves and the business. Everybody wins.

Now, let's talk about tech. The fitness world is going digital; if you're actively trying to keep up, you're falling behind. Being a tech-savvy leader isn't optional anymore - it's a necessity.

This doesn't mean you need to become a coding wizard overnight. But it means you need to understand how tech shapes our industry. AI, wearables, virtual training platforms - these aren't just buzzwords. They're tools that can supercharge your business if you know how to use them.

Lead by example. If you expect your team to embrace new tech, you must be at the forefront. Make learning and adaptation part of your culture. Stay curious, stay hungry for knowledge. The next big thing in fitness tech? Be there first. Do not create systems and processes you don't know how to use within your business. It may seem like a time suck, but you need to know how all the gears and pulleys in your engine operate or how are you going to find the issues and fix them? Take everyone else's word for it? You may not be a dictator, but you still need to be able to check everyone's work periodically. If you don't know how to use the CRM or other apps, how are you going to optimize them going forward?

And remember, all this tech gives us access to something invaluable: data. Use it to fuel your decisions. Implement systems that give you real-time insights into your business. As I've stated, in this game, informed decisions beat gut feelings every time.

Leadership isn't just about being the boss. It's about creating an environment where everyone becomes the best version of themselves. Do that, and you won't just have employees - you'll have a loyal team ready to help you conquer the fitness world.

Are you ready to stop being a boss and start being a leader? Your empire awaits. Let's get to work.

Reflection Questions:

1. Think about your current leadership style. How does it align with building a democratic business culture versus a dictatorial one? What specific behaviors or decisions reflect this?

2. Recall a time when you successfully motivated your team intrinsically. What did you do, and how did it impact your team's performance and morale?

3. How tech-savvy do you consider yourself as a leader? How has your technological knowledge (or lack thereof) affected your ability to lead and grow your business?

Action Steps:

1. Implement a weekly team feedback session. Create a safe space where your team can share ideas, concerns, and suggestions without fear of repercussion. Document the insights gained and create an action plan based on the feedback.

2. Choose one repetitive task in your business that you currently handle. Identify a team member who could take on this responsibility and create a plan to train and empower them to manage it independently.

3. Identify a new technology or tool that could benefit your coaching business. Spend at least two hours this week learning about it, then schedule a team meeting to discuss how you could implement it to improve your operations.

Chapter 14: Culture: Building a Fucking Empire, Not Just a Business

Let's discuss something that can make or break your fitness empire: culture. If you think culture is just some HR terminology, you're setting yourself up for failure.

Here's the deal: culture isn't just about having a ping-pong table in the break room or hosting monthly happy hours. It's the invisible force that drives your business forward or drags it into the ground. It's what makes your team show up every day ready to crush it or what makes them update their LinkedIn profiles on their lunch break.

You've spent years perfecting your coaching techniques, fine-tuning your marketing strategies, and building your client base. But if your company culture sucks, all of that hard work can quickly go to waste.

I've seen it happen. Coaches who build successful businesses on paper, but their team is miserable behind the curtain. The turnover rate is sky-high. Clients can feel the negative energy when they walk in the door or log into a virtual session. It's a ticking time bomb.

On the flip side, I've witnessed fitness businesses with rock-solid cultures absolutely dominate their markets. These are where team members are excited to work, ideas flow freely, and clients become raving fans. The secret? They've built more than just a business - they've created a community, a movement, an empire.

So, how do you build a culture that doesn't just support your business but propels it to new heights? It starts with trust.

Trust is the foundation of any strong culture. Without it, you're just a group working in the same space. With it, you're an unstoppable force. But here's the kicker: trust isn't given; it's earned. And as a leader, you need to earn it every day.

It means being transparent, even when it's uncomfortable. Did you miss your quarterly targets? Don't sugarcoat it. Lay it out for your team, explain what went wrong, and involve them in finding solutions. Be disappointed but don't come across angry. You'd be amazed at the ideas that can come from a team that feels trusted and valued.

But trust isn't just about sharing information. It's about creating an environment where people feel safe to take risks, speak up, and challenge the status quo. It's about fostering what's called "psychological safety." In plain English? It means your team isn't afraid to make mistakes or tell you about things that went wrong or aren't working.

I'm not talking about major errors that could tank the business. I'm talking about the mistakes that lead to growth and innovation. When your team knows they won't get their heads bitten off for trying something new and failing, they'll be more likely to come up with the ideas that catapult your business to the next level.

Remember, a culture of trust doesn't mean a culture without accountability. It means creating an environment where people hold themselves accountable because they care about the business and each other.

Next, let's discuss something often overlooked in the health and fitness world: human-centered design. What I mean is designing your business processes and systems with your team in mind.

Too often, we implement systems and processes that look great on paper but are a nightmare to use in real life. We force our teams to adapt to clunky software or convoluted workflows because that's what some consultant told us we should do, or we just plucked the biggest brand name from a Google search. If your systems are making your team's lives harder, they're not going to give you their best work.

Human-centered design means putting your team's needs at the center of your decision-making process. It means asking them what tools they need to do their jobs better. It means observing how they work and designing processes that enhance their productivity, not hinder it. You can still make the final decisions but now they are *more informed* decisions.

This isn't just some feel-good BS. It's about creating an environment where your team can do their best work. When your team is performing at its best, your business thrives.

Lastly, let's discuss creating an environment for greatness. I mean fostering an environment where creativity, innovation, and personal growth are encouraged and expected.

This means providing opportunities for your team to learn and grow. It means challenging them and supporting them with new responsibilities as they stretch their skills. It means recognizing and rewarding not only results but also effort and innovation.

You must also remember that motivating clients and those who work for you are very different things with different approaches. You can tell your clients to try harder, and they will get more out of the program. You can push them to put more effort into things because they will reap the rewards individually.

You cannot use the same style of leadership with your team. "You've got to just go harder" may come naturally to you as a coach, but it will eventually lead to resentment as a team leader. The rewards aren't the same thing. "Go harder for *your* rewards" and "Go harder for *my* rewards" ring a different bell in someone's head. The more you say the first one, the better people feel, whether or not the efforts are working. The more you emphasize the second one, whether or not it's working won't ultimately provide the same warm and fuzzy feeling that you are hoping it does over time.

Leaders lead. Coaches coach. Leaders can occasionally coach their teams. Coaches can be seen to lead. At the end of the day, don't confuse the two as fully interchangeable.

But here's the thing: creating this kind of culture isn't a one-and-done deal. It's not something you can install like a new piece of equipment. It's something you have to nurture every single day. It's in the way you communicate, the decisions you make, the way you respond (not react), and the behaviors you model.

Building a strong culture is hard work. It requires constant attention and care. But the payoff is worth it. When you get it right, you create more than just a successful business. You create a place where people want to work, where clients want to be, and where success is not just possible but inevitable.

So, are you ready to build a culture that turns your coaching business into an empire? It's time to roll up your sleeves and get to work. Your team, your clients, and your business will thank you.

Reflection Questions:

1. How would you describe your current company culture? Is it intentionally crafted or has it developed organically? How does it align with your vision for your coaching empire?

2. Think about a time when trust was broken in your business, either with a team member or a client. How did you handle it, and what did you learn about building a culture of trust from that experience?

3. In what ways are you currently applying (or not applying) human-centered design principles in your business processes and systems? How is this affecting your team's productivity and satisfaction?

Action Steps:

1. Conduct an *anonymous* culture survey with your team. Ask about trust, communication, work satisfaction, and areas for improvement. Review the results and identify one key area to focus on improving over the next month.

2. Implement a "culture of experimentation" initiative. Encourage your team to propose and test new ideas for improving processes or services. Set aside time in your next team meeting to brainstorm and select one idea to trial over the next two weeks.

3. Audit one of your key business processes (e.g., client onboarding, program design, or feedback collection) through the lens of human-centered design. Involve your team in redesigning this process better to serve both your team members and your clients.

Chapter 15: Crush Invisible Losses and Optimize Your Empire

You've built your team, established a killer culture, and your business is humming along. But here's the hard truth: you're probably bleeding money without even realizing it. Welcome to the world of invisible losses, the silent killers of coaching empires.

Wake Up to the Hidden Killers of Your Business

Let's start with a reality check. You're not as efficient as you think you are, and neither is your team. It's not because you're lazy or incompetent. It's because you're human, and humans are not good at seeing what's right in front of them unless they make a direct point to look for it.

Invisible losses are the small inefficiencies, the tiny time-wasters, the "that's just how we do things" processes that add up to major drags on your business. They're the meetings that could have been emails, the manual data entry that could be automated, the unnecessary spreadsheets, and the hours spent on social media that don't translate to new clients.

Here's the kicker: these losses aren't obvious. They don't show up as a line item on your expense report. But make no mistake– they're costing you. In time, in money, in missed opportunities. Time is money, period. Wherever you can save time, you can make more money
Take a hard look at your day. How much time do you spend on tasks that don't directly contribute to growing your business or serving your clients? Now multiply that across your entire team. Scary, isn't it?

But it's not just about time. It's about energy and focus, too. Every distraction, every context switch, and every unnecessary task is sapping your team's ability to do their best work. And in a business that's all about helping people transform their lives, anything less than your best is a disservice to your clients and your bottom line.

Optimization: Your Secret Weapon Against Invisible Losses

Now that you're aware of the problem let's discuss solutions. Optimization isn't just something business gurus use to sound cool; it's your secret weapon in the fight against invisible losses.

Start with your processes. Every single thing you do in your business should be questioned. Why do we do it this way? Is there a better way? Could this be automated? Could this be eliminated entirely? Are all of the processes properly documented so they can be fully analyzed? Is there data collected?

This isn't about cutting corners. It's about removing the fat so you can focus on your business's muscle. It's about working smarter, not just harder.

Look at your tech stack (the combination of different software systems, for the layman). Are your tools talking to each other, or are you wasting time needing a human bridge between systems? Are you using all the features you're paying for? Are there better options out there that could streamline your operations? Are there overlapping systems that have the same features, yet you're paying for both?

Don't forget about your team. Are they spending their time on high-value tasks or bogged down in busy work? Are they empowered to make decisions, or is everything bottlenecked, waiting for your approval?

Optimization is an ongoing process, not a one-time event. Make it a part of your company culture. Encourage your team to always look for better ways to do things. Reward efficiency and innovation.

The Future is Now: Embrace AI or Become Obsolete

Let's talk about the elephant in the room: AI. It's not coming; it's here. And it will either be your most powerful ally or the thing that makes you obsolete. The choice is yours.

AI isn't about replacing you or your team. It's about augmenting your capabilities, freeing you up to focus on what truly matters: the human connection at the heart of great coaching.

Imagine an AI that can analyze your clients' progress data and suggest personalized program adjustments. Or one that can handle your social media posting, freeing you up to actually engage with your audience. Or an AI that can draft your email responses, letting you communicate more effectively with more clients in less time. Or an AI chatbot knowledge base to answer the simple questions you and your team must constantly answer, such as, "How much of this should I eat on this day again?"

This isn't science fiction. These tools exist right now, and they're getting better every day. The coaches who learn to leverage AI will have a massive advantage over those who don't.

But here's the thing: AI is a tool, not a magic wand. It still needs human oversight, human creativity, and human empathy. Your job isn't to compete with AI; it's to use AI to become the best damn coach you can be. It's a tool you add to your toolbox to become a better overall performer.

Start small. Experiment with AI tools for content creation, data analysis, or customer service. Learn what works for your business and what doesn't. Stay curious. Stay adaptable.

I used AI tools to get this book from just an idea to being published in under 4 weeks by using AI tools. Did I have a robot write this for me? Not a chance. I used Perplexity for research. I used Claude and ChatGPT to organize my thoughts and ideas into outlines. I used Grammarly to make sure my grammar, spelling, and punctuation were all how they should be. This is what I mean by "tools in your toolbox". I saved weeks of Google Search research. I saved weeks, if not months, of structure building. I saved weeks of editing and proofreading. When you use AI as an assistant properly to amplify the speed of your thoughts and ideas, you're making yourself superhuman. Super, but still human.

The people out there strictly copying and pasting from AI are becoming increasingly obvious. Just don't be that person. You're a health or fitness coach. I don't see you as being lazy. Don't let me down on that one. You're doing yourself a disservice in the long run. People will pick up on it.

Remember, the goal isn't to replace the human element in your business. It's to use technology to enhance it, giving you and your team more time and energy to focus on what really matters: changing lives through fitness and health.

Crushing invisible losses, relentlessly optimizing, and embracing AI aren't just about increasing your profits (although they'll certainly do that). They're about building a resilient, adaptable business that is ready for whatever the future holds—always ready to scale and drive toward growth.

So, are you ready to stop the bleeding, streamline your empire, and step into the future of coaching? The time to act is now. Your business's survival depends on it.

Reflection Questions:

1. What are the biggest invisible losses in your business right now? How might addressing these impact your bottom line and overall efficiency?

2. In what ways are you currently leveraging AI in your coaching business? Where do you see the biggest opportunities for AI integration?

3. Think about your current optimization efforts. Are they focused more on technology or on human processes? How could you create a better balance?

Action Steps:

1. Conduct a time audit for one week. Track every task you do and categorize them as high-value or low-value. Identify three low-value tasks that could be eliminated, automated, or delegated.

2. Choose one AI tool relevant to your coaching business (e.g., for content creation, data analysis, or client communication). Implement it in your workflow and document the impact on your efficiency over the next two weeks.

3. Review your current tech stack. Identify any overlapping or underutilized tools. Create a plan to either fully leverage these tools or replace them with more efficient alternatives.

Chapter 16: The Pitfalls of Premature Scaling

You've got momentum. Your client list is growing, your team is crushing it, and you're starting to see some serious cash flow. It's tempting to think, "Hell yeah, let's blow this thing up!" But pump the brakes for a second. Scaling too fast too soon is like trying to sprint a marathon – you'll burn out before you hit your stride.

The Siren Song of Rapid Growth

Look, I get it. The allure of rapid growth is intoxicating. More clients, more revenue, more impact. But here's the cold, hard truth: premature scaling is one of the leading causes of business failure in the coaching industry.

You might be thinking, "But I've got demand! People want what I'm selling!" That's great, but can your business actually handle that growth? It's not just about whether you can get more clients – it's about whether you can properly serve them well while maintaining the quality that got you here in the first place.

Signs You're Not Ready to Scale

Let's do a reality check before you start dreaming about world domination. Here are some red flags that scream, "you're not ready to scale":

1. Your processes are held together with duct tape and prayers. If

you're still figuring things out on the fly, you're not ready to scale.

2. You're the bottleneck. If everything has to go through you, scaling will just create a bigger traffic jam. More people, more problems, only one of you.

3. Your team is already maxed out. If your current team is burning the candle at both ends, adding more clients will just burn down the whole house.

4. Your cash flow is inconsistent. Scaling requires investment. If you're living invoice to invoice, you're not ready.

5. You can't articulate your unique value proposition. If you don't know exactly what makes you different, how will you stand out in a bigger market?

The High Cost of Scaling Too Soon

Premature scaling isn't just a speed bump – it can be a business killer. Here's what's at stake:

1. Quality Nosedive:

More clients don't just mean more work—it means more complexity. If you're not ready, the quality of your coaching will suffer. And in this industry, your reputation is everything.

2. Team Burnout:

Pushing your team too hard, too fast is a one-way ticket to resignations and resentment. Good luck scaling when your best people are updating their resumes.

3. Financial Strain:

Scaling requires investment—in people, systems, and marketing. You could find yourself in a deep hole if you're not financially ready.

4. Lost Focus:

Rapid growth can pull you away from what made you successful in the first place. Suddenly, you're managing logistics instead of changing lives.

The Right Way to Scale

Alright, enough doom and gloom. Let's talk about how to scale the right way:

1. Nail Your Systems First:

Make sure your processes are rock solid before considering scaling. Document everything. Test everything. If it can't run without you, it's not ready to scale.

2. Build a Strong Foundation:

This means having the right team, technology, and financial reserves in place. Don't start building the second floor if your foundation is shaky.

3. Know Your Numbers:

I'm not just talking about revenue. Understand your customer acquisition cost, lifetime value, and churn rate—all of it. Data should drive your scaling decisions, not gut feelings. Definitely *not greed*.

4. Scale Incrementally:

You don't have to double in size overnight. Start with small, manageable growth. Test, learn, adjust, and then grow some more.

5. Keep Your Eye on Quality:

As you grow, obsess over maintaining the quality of your coaching. Your existing clients are your best marketing tool – don't let them down.

6. Invest in Your Team:

Scaling isn't just about adding more people—it's about developing the people you have. Invest in training, tools, and whatever they need to succeed at a larger scale. Do not think that just hiring more people means more profits. Another salesperson doesn't magically get more leads. Every aspect needs to be calculated and built based on data.

7. Stay True to Your Why:

Growth for the sake of growth is a recipe for disaster. Every scaling decision should align with your core purpose and values.

Remember, scaling isn't a race. It's not about who can get the biggest fastest. It's about building a sustainable, impactful business that can change more lives without sacrificing what made you great in the first place.

So before you hit the gas on growth, look hard at your business. Are you really ready to scale? Or do you need to shore up your foundation first? The future of your coaching empire depends on making the right call.

Don't let the excitement of potential growth blind you to the realities of scaling successfully. Be patient, be strategic, and, when the time is right, be unstoppable.

Reflection Questions:

1. Think about a time when you felt pressured to scale your business. What were the driving factors, and how did you respond? In hindsight, was it the right decision?

2. How would you rate your current systems and processes in terms of scalability? Which areas are most likely to become bottlenecks as you grow?

3. Consider your financial readiness for scaling. How many months of runway do you have? What investments would be necessary to scale effectively?

Action Steps:

1. Conduct a SWOT analysis (Strengths, Weaknesses, Opportunities, Threats) of your business as it stands today. Use this to identify areas that need strengthening before you consider scaling.

2. Choose one core process in your business (e.g., client onboarding, program delivery, or billing). Document this process in detail, then review it critically. Identify at least three ways you could optimize this process to make it more scalable.

3. Create a scaling checklist for your business. Include factors like financial stability, team capacity, systems robustness, and market demand. Use this to objectively assess your readiness to scale.

Chapter 17: Driving Growth Through Lead Generation and Sales

Alright, coach. You've got your systems in place, avoided the pitfalls of premature scaling, and are ready to grow. Now it's time to talk about the lifeblood of your business: leads and sales. Because let's face it, without a steady stream of new clients, you don't have a business – you have an expensive hobby.

I remember when I first started in the fitness industry. I thought my passion and skills were enough to bring clients flooding through the door. Boy, was I wrong. I quickly learned that being a great coach, being great at getting clients, and being great at closing sales are very different things.

Let's start with lead generation. You need a consistent flow of potential clients knocking on your virtual door. You can create funnels, you can run paid ads, you can do promo cycles, you can add in a referral bonus for existing clients, or a whole slew of other ways.

There is no way I could cover every option here effectively. It's another entire book's worth of content. You also need to figure out which way works best for you and your audience. If you want to get more in depth insight into the different approaches, join our free Facebook group (link at end of the book). There are very detailed guides that are focused on each lead generation option.

Now here's the kicker—not all leads are created equal. You don't just need more leads; you need the right leads—people who are ready, willing, and *able to invest* in their health and fitness.

Yes, you want you and/or your sales team to get at-bats. You want a fully filled sales call schedule. The key is that you don't want to fill up the sales call schedule with anybody who raises their hand. You need to qualify people. Don't waste your resources and team's time on people who can't afford your services.

You are high-level. You charge high-level prices. You can direct the people who don't qualify to your low ticket offers to give them value and to build trust. One day they might be able to invest. If that day isn't today? They shouldn't be on the calendar in hopes you or your closer can bend over backwards pulling magic out of their ass to make it work.

The key to effective lead generation is understanding your ideal client inside and out. I'm not talking about superficial demographics here. I mean, really getting into their heads. What keeps them up at night? What have they tried before? Why did it fail? The better you understand your ideal client, the more effectively you can target them.

Once you know who you're targeting, it's time to create content that speaks directly to them. And I'm not talking about generic "5 tips for six-pack abs" bullshit. I'm talking about content that actually solves problems for your ideal clients. Make it so good they can't help but want more.

In the fitness world, results talk. Showcase your clients'

transformations, but don't just focus on the physical—highlight the mental and emotional transformations, too. People want to see themselves in your success stories. Also, do not fill your feed nonstop with client transformations. Use it, but don't overuse it. It can become redundant to prospective clients.

Time to Close Sales

Now, let's talk about the elephant in the room: sales. I know, I know. You got into coaching to help people, not to be a "salesperson." But here's the truth: if you can't sell your services, you can't help anyone. Period.

The first step to becoming good at sales is to shift your mindset. You're not "selling" – you're offering a solution to someone's problem. If you truly believe in what you offer, selling is an act of service.

I learned this lesson the hard way. I used to feel awkward and pushy when trying to close a sale. I felt bad pulling on the strings of people's most intense pain points. But then I realized something: if I truly believed that I could help this person transform their life, wasn't I doing them a disservice by not convincing them to work with my team?

The best salespeople are the best listeners. The best at asking the right questions at the right time. Understand your potential client's needs, fears, and goals before you make an offer, and tailor your offer based on what you've learned.

"One-size-fits-all" doesn't work in fitness, and it doesn't work in sales.

Don't be afraid to address objections head-on. In fact, anticipate them and address them proactively. Is the price too high? Explain the value. No time? Show how you'll make it fit their schedule. Hit every objection with a question. If they think the price is too high then ask them why. If they don't think it will work for them then ask them why. When people have to repeat their "why" you can begin to frame it as "just another excuse" to not reach their goals.

You're going to hurt some feelings. Good. Today's society has unintelligently pushed a culture of avoiding hurting anyone's feelings. People only make changes when they feel bad about something. If humans don't feel bad then they have zero motivation for growth. Hurting feelings without being insulting is an art. It isn't easy. You don't want to be an asshole but you want to create a drive for change. Hold a mirror up to people's bullshit. Their current state isn't acceptable. They wouldn't be talking to you if it was.

People will also try to minimize their situation. "I am *only* 30 pounds overweight." is one way people will approach their pain to make themselves subconsciously accept their shortcomings. It's your job to *maximize* the pain they are minimizing. Hold the mirror in front of their face with your words. "Only 30 pounds?! That isn't a small task. That's a lot. You don't think that's a lot?" Don't let people talk themselves out of changing for the better. Change their lives for them. Give them the push. Never feel bad about it. You're helping them. They currently aren't. Period.

Remember, most sales aren't made on the first contact. Have a solid follow-up system in place. But there's a fine line between persistent and pestering—learn to walk away when they aren't interested.

Now, let's talk about scaling your lead gen and sales efforts. You can't be everywhere at once and shouldn't try to be. This is where automation comes in. Email marketing, chatbots, CRM systems – can all help you manage leads and nurture relationships at scale.

But remember, automation is a tool, not a replacement for human connection. Use it to handle the repetitive stuff so you can focus on what matters: having meaningful conversations with potential clients.

Here's the thing about lead generation and sales: it's never done. Markets change, platforms evolve, and what worked yesterday might not work tomorrow. Stay curious, keep testing, and never stop learning.

Your ability to consistently generate leads and convert them into clients will make or break your coaching business. Being a great coach is not enough—you need to be great at getting your services in front of the right people and convincing them to take action.

So, are you ready to become a lead gen and sales machine? Your empire awaits. Let's get to work.

Reflection Questions:

1. Analyze your current lead generation strategy. Which channels are most effective for your business? Are there any untapped opportunities you've been overlooking?

2. Think about your sales process. Where do you feel most confident, and where do you struggle? How does this align with your values as a coach?

3. Consider your approach to follow-ups. How persistent are you? Have you ever lost a potential client because you gave up too soon or pushed too hard?

Action Steps:

1. Create a detailed ideal client avatar. Include demographics, psychographics, pain points, and goals. Use this to craft a piece of content specifically targeted at this ideal client and share it on your primary marketing channel.

2. Review your last 10 sales calls. Identify common objections and create a "swipe file" of effective responses. Practice these responses until they feel natural and authentic.

3. Implement one new automation in your lead generation or sales process. This could be setting up an email nurture sequence, using a chatbot for initial inquiries, or creating a system for automated follow-ups. Monitor its effectiveness over the next

month.

Download the free printable PDF workbook with ALL the Action Steps, additional guides, templates and MORE:

http://engineforimpact.com/workbook

Chapter 18: Sustainable Growth and Building a Resilient Coaching Business

You've come a long way, coach. You've built your empire from the ground up, navigated the treacherous waters of scaling, and mastered the art of lead generation and sales. But here's the million-dollar question: Can you keep it up?

Sustainable growth isn't just about getting bigger; it's about getting better. It's about building a business that can weather any storm, adapt to any change, and continue to thrive year after year. And let me tell you, in an industry as dynamic and competitive as online health and fitness coaching, that's no small feat.

I remember when I first hit what I thought was "success" in this business. I had a full call schedule, money flowed in, and I worked around the clock. I thought I'd made it. But you know what? I was miserable. I was stressed, exhausted, and one bad month away from it all falling apart. That's when I realized that what I had wasn't success – it was a ticking time bomb.

Real success, sustainable success, is about more than just numbers on a spreadsheet. It's about building a business that serves you, not the other way around. It's about creating systems and structures that allow you to grow without sacrificing your sanity or passion for coaching.

So, how do you build a business that's not just successful but sustainable? It starts with diversification. If all your eggs are in one basket – like one-on-one coaching – you're setting yourself up for burnout and stagnation. Diversify your offerings. Group coaching, online courses, digital products – these aren't just additional revenue streams— they're safety nets.

But here's the catch: diversification without focus is just a distraction. You can't be everything to everyone. Choose your lanes carefully, and make sure each new offering aligns with your core mission and values. Remember why you started this journey in the first place.

Staying Power

Next, let's talk about resilience. In the world of fitness, we know that the strongest bodies can adapt to any challenge. The same is true for businesses. A resilient business isn't one that never faces setbacks—it's one that can bounce back stronger every time.

Building resilience starts with your mindset. Embrace challenges as opportunities for growth. When I lost a major client early in my coaching sales career, I didn't see it as a failure – I saw it as a chance to reassess my approach and come back stronger. And you know what? That setback led to one of the biggest breakthroughs in my own business later down the line. I remembered what I learned earlier in this industry and was able to apply it as I got my own coaching business off the ground.

Resilience also means having the right systems in place. Solid financial management, diverse revenue streams, and a strong team are your shock absorbers when the road gets rough. And trust me, the road will get rough. The question isn't if challenges will come but when.

Let's talk about your team for a moment. Sustainable growth isn't a solo sport. You need a team that's not just skilled but aligned with your vision. As I've mentioned, invest in your people. Train them, empower them, trust them. A strong team can weather any storm, and they'll take your business places you never dreamed possible. If you can't trust your people to do things correctly, you hired the wrong people.

But even with the best team in the world, you can't neglect your own growth. The fitness industry is constantly evolving, and you need to evolve with it. Stay curious. Keep learning. Attend conferences, read voraciously, and network with other successful coaches. Your business can only grow as much as you do.

Now, let's address the elephant in the room: work-life balance. I know it sounds like some new-age BS. But hear me out. Sustainable growth isn't just about your business – it's about you. If you're burning the candle at both ends, eventually, you'll burn out. And when you burn out, your business burns with you.

I learned this lesson the hard way. I used to wear my 80-hour workweeks like a badge of honor. But you know what? My relationships suffered, my health suffered, and, ironically, my business suffered, too. When you're exhausted and stressed, you can't show up as your best self for your clients, staff, and loved ones.

Create boundaries. Schedule time for self-care. Delegate. Automate. Do whatever you need to do to create space in your life. A sustainable business allows you to have a life outside of work.

Lastly, never lose sight of your impact. In the day-to-day grind of running a business, it's easy to forget why you started coaching in the first place. But your impact—the lives you change, the transformations you facilitate—is the real measure of your success.

Building a sustainable, resilient coaching business isn't easy. It requires hard work, smart planning, and a willingness to adapt. But the payoff? A business that not only survives but thrives. A business that allows you to make the impact you've always dreamed of without sacrificing your own well-being in the process.

So, coach, are you ready to build a business that stands the test of time? Are you ready to create something that's not just successful but sustainable? The journey doesn't end here – in many ways, it's just beginning. But with the right mindset, the right strategies, and an unwavering commitment to your mission, there's no limit to what you can achieve.

Your resilient, sustainable empire awaits. Let's build it to last.

Reflection Questions:

1. How would you define "sustainable growth" for your coaching business? What specific metrics or indicators would show that you're achieving it?

2. Think about a recent challenge or setback in your business. How did you respond? What did this experience teach you about your business's resilience?

3. Consider your work-life balance. How has it evolved as your business has grown? What changes must you make to ensure your personal growth is sustainable?

Action Steps:

1. Conduct a revenue stream analysis. Identify all your current income sources and their relative contributions. Brainstorm at least two new potential revenue streams that align with your core mission and expertise.

2. Create a personal development plan for the next six months. Include goals for your physical health, mental wellbeing, and professional skills. Schedule specific times in your calendar to work on these goals.

3. Organize a brainstorming session on building resilience. Identify potential future challenges and develop contingency plans. Use this to create a "resilience roadmap" for your business.

Conclusion: Your Roadmap to Coaching Success

Well, coach, we've been through one hell of a journey together. From laying the foundation of your coaching mindset to building a resilient, sustainable empire, we've covered a lot of ground. But here's the thing – this isn't the end. It's just the beginning.

Remember when you first started your coaching business? The fire in your belly, the vision of changing lives, the dream of building something meaningful? I hope that the fire's still burning bright. If there's one thing I want you to take away from this book, it's this: Your passion for coaching, combined with the strategies we've discussed, makes your business an unstoppable force.

We've discussed many different aspects of building a successful coaching business. We've dug into the nitty-gritty of systems and processes, explored the art of scaling without losing your soul, and tackled the challenges of lead generation and sales. But at the core of it all is you—the coach, the visionary, the empire builder.

Your journey as a coach and a business owner is unique. There's no one-size-fits-all formula for success. What works for one coach might not work for another. That's why taking what we've discussed in this book and making it your own is crucial. Adapt, twist, and shape it to fit your vision and *your* business goals.

Remember, building a coaching empire isn't just about making money (although that's certainly a nice perk). It's about impact. It's about leaving your mark on the world. Every client you help, every life you transform, ripples out into the world in ways you might never see. Never lose sight of that impact.

As you move forward, there will be challenges. There will be days when you question everything and wonder if it's all worth it. On those days, remember why you started. Remember the lives you've changed. Remember the empire you're building.

Stay hungry, stay curious. The fitness industry is always evolving, and so should you. Keep learning, keep growing, and keep pushing your limits. Your business can only grow as much as you do.

Embrace failure as a teacher. Every setback is an opportunity to learn, to grow, and to come back stronger. The most successful coaches aren't the ones who never fail – they're the ones who never give up.

Build a team that shares your vision. Surround yourself with people who believe in what you're doing and who push you to be better. Remember, no empire was ever built alone.

Take care of yourself. Your business needs you at your best. Prioritize your physical and mental health. Set boundaries. Make time for the things that matter outside of work. A burnt-out coach can't change lives.

And above all, stay true to your why. In pursuing growth and success, it's easy to lose sight of why you started coaching in the first place. Don't let that happen. Let your purpose be your North Star, guiding every decision you make.

You have everything you need to build a coaching empire that changes lives and leaves a lasting impact on the world. The strategies, mindset, and passion are all there. Now it's time to take action.

So, coach, are you ready? Are you ready to step up, push past your limits, and build something truly extraordinary? Are you ready to turn your coaching business into an empire that will stand the test of time?

The world needs what you have to offer. Your future clients are out there waiting for you to show up and change their lives. Don't keep them waiting.

Your empire awaits. Now, go and build it.

- Make sure to join our free community for coaches looking to take their business to the next level:
  https://www.facebook.com/groups/engineforimpact
- Follow me on Instagram for more value:
  https://www.instagram.com/joeoliveimpact/
- Find me on Facebook:
  https://www.facebook.com/joeolive.impact
- Find me on LinkedIn:
  https://www.linkedin.com/in/joe-olive-24537b295/
- Visit our website for more products and services like this:
  https://engineforimpact.com/

Appendix: Essential Resources for Online Health and Fitness Coaches

A. Business Management Tools

Customer Relationship Management (CRM) Systems

- **HubSpot CRM**: A comprehensive CRM platform offering robust free tools for managing contacts and sales pipelines.
- **Salesforce**: Highly customizable CRM solutions suitable for larger coaching businesses looking for advanced features.
- **Zoho CRM**: Affordable and scalable CRM with automation capabilities and extensive integrations.
- **TrueCoach**: Specifically designed for fitness coaches, offering tools for workout delivery, client communication, and progress tracking.

Project Management Tools

- **Asana**: A versatile tool for managing tasks, projects, and team collaboration.
- **Trello**: Visual project management using boards, lists, and cards, ideal for organizing coaching programs.
- **ClickUp**: An all-in-one project management platform that can handle tasks, docs, goals, and more.
- **Monday.com**: Customizable workflows to streamline team management and project tracking.

Scheduling and Booking Software

- **Calendly**: Simple scheduling automation to eliminate back-and-forth emails.
- **Acuity Scheduling**: Comprehensive scheduling tool with client self-scheduling and payment processing.
- **BookSteam**: Online scheduling software that supports group bookings and classes.
- **MindBody**: Robust booking and management software tailored for fitness businesses, integrating client management and marketing tools.

B. Marketing and Content Creation Resources

Email Marketing Platforms

- **Mailchimp**: User-friendly email marketing with extensive templates and automation features.
- **ConvertKit**: Designed for creators, offering powerful automation and tagging systems.
- **ActiveCampaign**: Advanced email marketing with CRM and automation capabilities.
- **Klaviyo**: Ideal for e-commerce businesses, offering robust segmentation and personalization.

Social Media Management Tools

- **Hootsuite**: Manage multiple social media accounts, schedule posts, and track performance.
- **Buffer**: Simplified social media scheduling and analytics.
- **Later**: Visual scheduling tool for Instagram and other social

platforms.
- **Sprout Social**: Comprehensive social media management with robust analytics and reporting.

Graphic Design Tools

- **Canva**: Easy-to-use design tool with templates for social media, presentations, and more.
- **Adobe Creative Suite**: Professional design software for creating high-quality visuals.
- **Snapseed**: Mobile photo editing app with advanced editing tools.
- **Visme**: Tool for creating infographics, presentations, and visual content.

Video Creation and Editing Tools

- **iMovie**: User-friendly video editing software for Mac users.
- **DaVinci Resolve**: Professional video editing software with advanced features.
- **Filmora**: Accessible video editing with a wide range of effects and templates.
- **Lumen5**: Turn blog posts and articles into engaging video content.
- **Capcut:** Best video editing software for the money. Mobile and desktop versions available.

C. Online Learning Platforms for Continuous Education

- **Coursera**: Access to courses from top universities and institutions worldwide.
- **edX**: Online learning platform offering courses from leading universities.
- **Udemy**: Wide range of courses on various topics, including fitness and business.
- **LinkedIn Learning**: Professional development courses and certifications.
- **MasterClass**: Learn from industry experts and thought leaders.

D. Fitness Industry-Specific Resources

- **ACE (American Council on Exercise)**: Certification programs and continuing education for fitness professionals.
- **NASM (National Academy of Sports Medicine)**: Certification and specialization courses for fitness trainers.
- **ISSA (International Sports Sciences Association)**: Comprehensive fitness education and certification.
- **Precision Nutrition**: Leading certification program for nutrition coaching.

E. Business Coaching and Development

- **Engine for Impact**: Specialized business coaching for health and fitness professionals.
- **Small Business Administration (sba.gov)**: Resources

and support for small business owners.
- **SCORE**: Free business mentoring and education for entrepreneurs.

F. Financial Management Tools

- **QuickBooks**: Accounting software for small to medium-sized businesses.
- **FreshBooks**: Cloud accounting software with invoicing and time tracking.
- **Wave**: Free financial software for small businesses with accounting, invoicing, and payroll.
- **Xero**: Online accounting software with real-time financial data.

G. Legal Resources

- **LegalZoom**: Online legal services for business formation and legal documents.
- **Rocket Lawyer**: Legal documents and lawyer consultations.
- **NOLO**: Legal encyclopedia and resources for small businesses.

H. Networking and Community Building

- **LinkedIn Groups for Fitness Professionals**: Engage with industry peers and share knowledge.
- **Facebook Groups for Online Coaches**: Join communities

of coaches for support and networking.
- **Professional Associations**: IDEA Health & Fitness Association, American College of Sports Medicine (ACSM), and others provide networking and professional development opportunities.

I. Podcasts for Health and Fitness Entrepreneurs

- **The Fitness Business Podcast**: Insights and strategies from fitness industry leaders.
- **The Online Trainer Show**: Tips and advice for running a successful online training business.
- **The Business of Fitness**: Interviews with successful fitness professionals on business strategies.
- **Fitness Marketing Mastery**: Marketing strategies specifically for fitness professionals.

J. Recommended Books

- **"The E-Myth Revisited" by Michael E. Gerber**: Understanding and overcoming the myths about starting and growing a business.
- **"Building a StoryBrand" by Donald Miller**: Clarifying your message to create effective marketing.
- **"The Lean Startup" by Eric Ries**: Innovative approach to business startups and product development.
- **"Atomic Habits" by James Clear**: Strategies for building good habits and breaking bad ones.

- **"Oversubscribed" by Daniel Priestley**: Creating demand and positioning your business for success.

K. Wellness and Self-Care Resources

- **Headspace**: Meditation app for mindfulness and stress relief.
- **Calm**: App for meditation, sleep, and relaxation.
- **Insight Timer**: Free meditation app with guided sessions.
- **Blinkist**: Book summary app for continuous learning and personal development.

L. Technology for Virtual Coaching

- **Zoom**: Video conferencing tool for virtual coaching sessions.
- **Google Meet**: Free video meetings for coaching and group sessions.
- **Skype**: Reliable video calling for virtual coaching.
- **Microsoft Teams**: Collaboration platform with video conferencing capabilities.

M. Fitness Tracking and Progress Monitoring Apps

- **MyFitnessPal**: Calorie counting and diet tracking app.
- **Fitbit**: Activity tracking and health monitoring.
- **Apple Health**: Comprehensive health tracking for Apple

users.
- **Strava**: GPS-based app for tracking running and cycling activities.

N. Online Course Creation Platforms

- **Teachable**: Create and sell online courses with an easy-to-use platform.
- **Thinkific**: Build and market online courses with comprehensive tools.
- **Kajabi**: All-in-one platform for creating and marketing online courses.
- **Podia**: Simple platform for creating online courses and digital products.

www.ingramcontent.com/pod-product-compliance
Lightning Source LLC
Chambersburg PA
CBHW071924210526
45479CB00002B/548